WaxPoetics

ISSUE 67

CONTRIBUTING WRITERS
A. D. AMOROSI
ERICKA BLOUNT DANOIS
DAN DODDS
MICHAEL A. GONZALES
DEAN VAN NGUYEN
CHRIS WILLIAMS

CONTRIBUTING PHOTOGRAPHERS
JOE GIANNETTI
DEAN MESSINA
DEBRA TREBITZ

EDITOR BRIAN DIGENTI
MARKETING DIRECTOR DENNIS COXEN
ASSOCIATE EDITOR TOM MCCLURE
CONTRIBUTING EDITOR CHRIS WILLIAMS
EDITOR-AT-LARGE ANDREW MASON

FRONT COVER
COURTESY OF WARNER BROS.
BACK COVER
BY DEBRA TREBITZ (1985) / FRANK WHITE AGENCY

ISBN 978-0-9992127-2-1
© 2018 WAX POETICS

PUBLISHED BY WAX POETICS BOOKS, SPRING 2018.
PRINTED BY LIGHTNING SOURCE.

Prince at the Lakeland Civic Center in Lakeland, Florida, April 5, 1985. Photo by Dean Messina / Frank White Agency.

A gallery of Prince record art.

THE BEAUTIFUL ONES

(*opposite*) Cover of *Around the World in a Day* by Prince and the Revolution, released on Paisley Park in 1985. Cover painting by Doug Henders.

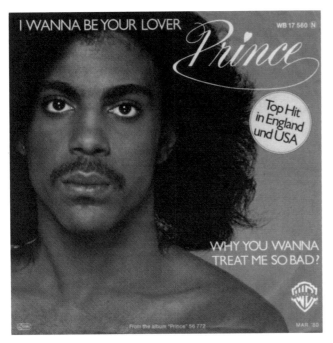

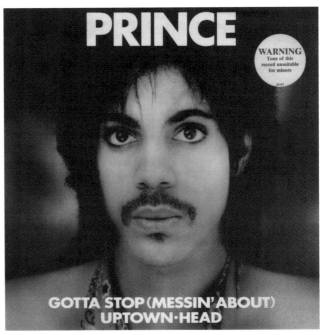

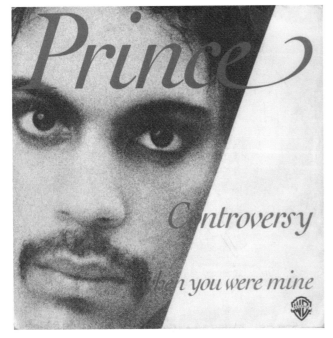

PRINCE
★★1999★★
PRODUCED, ARRANGED, COMPOSED
AND PERFORMED* BY PRINCE

RECORD ONE
1-23720

1

1. 1999 · 6:22
2. LITTLE RED CORVETTE · 4:58
3. DELIRIOUS · 3:56

All songs published by Controversy Music ASCAP
© 1982 Warner Bros. Records Inc. for the U.S. & WEA
International Inc. for the world outside of the U.S.
℗ 1982 Warner Bros. Records Inc. for the U.S. & WEA
International Inc. for the world outside of the U.S.
A Warner Communications Company

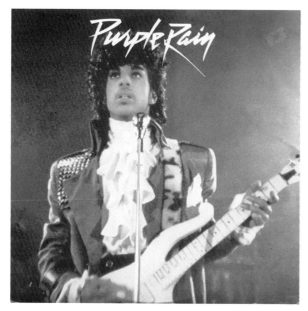

Paintings by Doug Henders.

(*above*) Inner sleeve of *Sign "O" the Times* by Prince, released on Paisley Park in 1987. Photo by Jeff Katz.

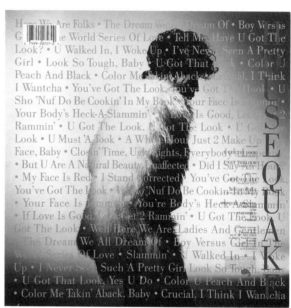

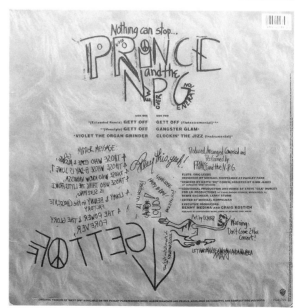

THE
CREATOR
HAD A
MASTER
PLAN

PRELUDE

by Chris Williams

Prince Rogers Nelson is regarded as one of the most inventive musicians in the history of music. For the past four decades, he draped the world in his trademark purple sheen through his ubiquitous, charismatic influence, which elevated the sound of American popular music. With thirty-nine solo albums and a host of unreleased material to his credit, as well as numerous producing contributions to the discography of legendary artists, Prince left an indelible mark on the ears and hearts he touched through his unparalleled musicianship. Simply put, he belongs on the Mount Rushmore of musicians. While growing up in rural Virginia, my earliest memory of hearing Prince was watching *Batman* at a local movie theater in 1989. I was eight years old. Two years later, when I finally had access to cable, I saw him on BET in his video for "Diamonds and Pearls." At the time, my musical palate consisted of New Jack Swing, Michael Jackson, and gospel music. This song captured my attention due to its beautiful arrangement and Rosie Gaines's powerhouse vocals. Truth be told, it took me until my late teens to dig into his vast catalog. Once I did more digging, I became a proud member of the Purple Army.

By the time Prince was seven years old, he had written his first song entitled "Funk Machine," a precursor of things to come. As he continued his musical journey, he honed his prodigious gifts of mastering multiple instruments, songwriting, composing, producing, and arranging. During his teenage years, he would participate in various local groups, such as 94 East and Grand Central (who later changed their name to Champagne). While working with Champagne in 1976, Prince met Chris Moon, the person who would enhance his skill set and introduce him to his future manager, Owen Husney. After meeting Moon and Husney, Prince's music career was about to take full flight. Under their tutelage, he landed a recording contract with Warner Bros. Records. Dubbed as the next Stevie Wonder by the brass at the record label, Prince was just starting to get his feet wet, but he was in total command of his craft by his late teenage years.

When he arrived on the scene in 1978 with his debut offering, *For You*, he was on the verge of becoming a wunderkind. Shortly thereafter, his wunderkind status was cemented with the releasing of his 1979 self-titled sophomore effort. As the new decade beckoned, he raised his creative bar and pushed the proverbial envelope, by showcasing more sexual and political themes, intertwined with a cosmic fusion of musical genres, ranging from rock and roll to funk. During this juncture, he incorporated his backup band, and after a couple lineup substitutions, he eventually named them the Revolution. With Prince serving as the ethereal conductor, he turned the music world on top of its head and proceeded to dominate the first half of the 1980s, with a string of eclectic, influential albums: *Dirty Mind* (1980), *Controversy* (1981), *1999* (1982), *Purple Rain* (1984), and *Around the World in a Day* (1985). The only musician who maintained a similar rigorous, torrid pace of recording and producing his own material and for other artists was Stevie Wonder from 1971 to 1976. While spearheading the creation of the aforementioned albums, not to mention starring in the film *Purple Rain*, Prince managed to find time to produce songs under the aliases Jamie Starr, the Starr Company, Joey Coco, Alexander Nevermind, Christopher, and Christopher Tracy for numerous artists, such as the Time, Sheila E., Vanity 6, and Apollonia 6, among many others.

By 1986, Prince had become an international phenomenon due to his prolific output of high-quality artistry. In an effort to continue experimenting with his sound, he decided to switch gears and follow the same blueprint as *Purple Rain*, by using his next album as the soundtrack for his next movie, *Under the Cherry Moon*. *Parade* became his fourth consecutive multiplatinum-selling album. As it turned out, this would be the last album he utilized his trademark band, the Revolution, which signaled a new direction for him in the coming years. A year later, he recorded his magnum opus, *Sign "O" the Times*. Initially, the material for the album spawned from three different album concepts: *Camille*, *Crystal Ball*, and *Dream Factory*. Prince pushed his record label to release a triple album, but they forced him to relent and downsize to release his second double album. As a result, it became another overwhelming smash and placed him in another league of his own. For the remainder of the decade, he released two more albums: 1988's *Lovesexy*, his least successful album since *1999*—yet still going gold within the year—and a soundtrack for Tim Burton's 1989 smash film *Batman*. Within the same time span, he constructed another band called the New Power Generation. At the beginning of the 1990s, Prince was starting to feel the impact of hip-hop and knew that the marketplace was trending in the genre's favor. In 1990, he returned to the blueprint he'd previously laid out with *Purple Rain*, by releasing his *Graffiti Bridge* album to accompany another film with the same title. The following year, he released *Diamonds and Pearls*. This album saw Prince experimenting with hip-hop by featuring an MC named Tony M., and showcasing his backing band the New Power Generation. It became another commercial breakthrough for Prince.

In an effort to delve deeper into Prince's classic catalog, I've spoken to producer/engineer Chris Moon, manager Owen Husney, producer/engineer David "David Z" Rivkin, producer/engineer Susan Rogers, bassist/guitarist/producer Levi Seacer Jr., and engineer Michael Koppelman about their involvement in the construction of four albums: 1978's *For You*, 1986's *Parade*, 1987's *Sign "O" the Times*, and 1991's *Diamonds and Pearls*. These albums encompass three different decades in Prince's iconic career, including his early days as a recording artist.

Other Wax Poetics writers help fill in some of the gaps by taking a look at the albums *Lovesexy* (1988), *The Gold Experience* (1995), and Prince protégé and singer Jill Jones's 1987 solo record on Paisley Park. We also speak to friend and early collaborator André Cymone and the other members of his seminal group, the Revolution—keyboardist Matt "Doctor" Fink, keyboardist Lisa Coleman, guitarist Wendy Melvoin, bassist Brown Mark, and drummer Bobby Z.—who, in some form, participated in the classic albums *Dirty Mind* (1980), *Controversy* (1981), *1999* (1982), *Purple Rain* (1984), *Around the World in a Day* (1985), and *Parade*.

Our story of the Almighty Purple One begins on the North Side of Minneapolis, Minnesota.

(*opposite*) Photo by Jurgen Reisch, courtesy of Warner Bros. As seen on 1979's *Prince*.
(*previous spread*) Photography by Joe Giannetti, courtesy of Warner Bros. As seen on the inner sleeve of 1978's *For You*.

At just eighteen years of age, Prince self-produced his debut album, 1978's FOR YOU, writing all the music and playing every instrument himself. Two years prior, Prince, already a multi-instrumentalist wunderkind, met studio owner/engineer Chris Moon, who would change his life by teaching him the ins and outs of recording while also helping him to find his voice and style. With a demo in hand, Moon delivered him to Owen Husney, who would manage the young artist and score a record deal with Warner Bros., setting into motion a historic musical career from a creative force of nature.

THE MASTER

by Chris Williams

When and where did you first meet Prince?

Chris Moon: I had a recording studio in South Minneapolis in the 1970s. The name of the studio was Moon Sound Studios. It would be fair to say it was the only studio in town that was really doing mostly Black music and R&B. The reason I was doing mostly R&B was because it was the kind of music I liked. I am an Englishman from England, originally, but I was always drawn by the joy that R&B and Black-rooted music brought more than anything else. Sixty percent of my time was given away to local bands. So if I found somebody I liked, I'd just bring them into the studio and record them, produce them, and put it all together. There was never any charges for the artists. I did that because one of the reasons I had a recording studio is because I liked music. Most people start recording studios because they are trying to make money and like music. [*laughs*] I was fairly known in Minneapolis. If you were a Black artist, it was the studio to go to. There were a couple other studios, but they were doing mostly rock and country and things like that. A band called Champagne booked some time at my studio to put together a demo tape. It was actually a paying gig. One of the band members' mothers was managing the band because it was all young kids who were fifteen, sixteen, and seventeen years old. She booked some time with me to do a demo tape.

So they were recording in the studio. Each day at lunchtime, the band would break and go across the street to Baskin-Robbins to get an ice cream cone, and I would sit in the control room eating my lunch. One day while I was sitting there eating my lunch, I looked out into the studio and one of the artists stayed behind. The one that stayed behind was Prince. He started playing on the piano. I kept eating my sandwich, and a bit later I looked up and he was over there playing the guitar. A bit longer I looked up and he was over there playing the drums. I looked up again and he was over there playing the bass. [*laughs*] And I said, "That's interesting. It looks like he can play all the instruments." It finally occurred to me, I was spending all this time giving time away to artists and recording other musicians. I needed to record some of my own material. I'd been a songwriter since I was thirteen or something, so I had a lot of songs put together. I wanted to produce my music, but I realized working with bands was one of the nightmares in life. One of the...things I'd become acutely aware of with a recording studio was the incredible difficulty involved in getting a band to all show up at the same time at the same place, and then do that on a regular basis.

So I was sitting there thinking, "Okay, I want to record some of my own material, and I don't really want to work with a band, but what other options do I have?" And then I see Prince at the studio running around playing different instruments and I'm thinking, "There may be the solution to my problem. Now, all I got to do is to get one guy to show up. If he played all the instruments, wouldn't that be great." So after the session that day, I walked right up to him. He and I had probably not said more than two sentences to one another. He was incredibly shy. I mean, he just didn't speak. I walked up to him and said, "Look, I'm looking to produce some original material. I would like to make you the artist. I will build a demo tape around you. I will package you up and write some songs for you, and I will teach you how to record and produce in the studio and see if I can make you famous. What do you think?" He looked up to me and said, "Yeah!" I reached in my pocket, and I handed him the keys to my recording studio, which was everything I owned in my life because I was only nineteen. I handed him the keys and he looked at me, and I said to myself, "You have just handed the keys to this small kid from the North Side of town that you don't even know." I said to him, "Meet me here tomorrow after school. Take the bus over after school. I'll be working. I'll leave two songs on the piano. Pick your favorite song and develop the music. When I get back, I'll teach you how to record it. We'll put some songs together." That's how it started.

When you began working with him on your material, what were those first sessions like?

Moon: Okay, so, this one should be pretty interesting, because it's surprising how few people reach out to get the beginning of Prince, because I've maintained that Prince was born in my studio. I'm not maintaining I made him—but I'm maintaining he was born in the studio. And after you're done with this interview, I think you'll agree. So he would come over—a shy, little, and quiet, five-feet-four-inch kid with an Afro from the North Side of town—and let himself into the studio and pick one of the two sets of lyrics I'd left on the piano. He'd work them up and then I'd show up. I was working at an ad agency back then, so I was learning about advertising, marketing, sales, and all of that. I'd show up to the studio and we'd sit down, and he'd play some music on the piano or guitar, typically. Then we'd start singing the lyrics together until we could work up the melody. And then we started recording it. He had never been in the studio before, so this was all new to him. I started teaching him how to record things, how tracks worked, and how to layer tracks. We got through building up our first song. We spent quite a bit of time working on it. Then, we spent quite a bit of time getting him used to the studio and recording the music to this first song. We were maybe a month into the process, and it was time to lay down the vocals on our first song.

He was in the studio, and I was in the control room. He had the headphones on. I started playing the music. It was coming over the headphones. I looked out into the room. I saw his lips moving as the song was playing, and I looked down at my meters and they weren't moving, and I couldn't hear anything. I'm thinking, "Okay, I've got a bad mic or a bad cord." So I went into the studio. I swapped the mic out, came back, still nothing. Okay, obviously, it was the cord. I went back, and I swapped the cord out. I came back again and still nothing. Over the course of ten minutes or so, I troubleshot all that equipment because I saw him singing but nothing was picking up. Then, it occurred to me, I went to the door while the track was playing, and I saw him singing and I stuck my head in the studio and I couldn't hear anything. I walked over to him and he stopped. I said, "Keep singing. Keep singing." And I realized that he was singing so softly that I could hardly even hear him.

I said, "Prince, Prince, Prince, you're not singing loud enough. I thought that I had a technical problem here. The problem is, I need some volume out of you, man. I can't even hear you. The mic can't pick you up." I had sensitive mics. Then we started this process of trying to get him to sing louder. He couldn't. I don't know whether it was shyness or intimidation or being scared or whatever. I started looking at his psychological profile to better understand. I had a five-feet-four-inch Black guy who always wanted to be a basketball player. That dream wasn't going to happen. It just wasn't going to happen. I had a five-feet-four-inch, Afro-haired Black dude whose name was Prince, and everyone at school was calling him Princess. They were beating him up because he was short and little. Now, he's going to break out singing in a falsetto girl's voice. When I started putting it together like that, I started to realize that the dude was facing some intimidation issues from life. I thought, "Shit, I've got a problem here. I've got all this time invested in my hand-selected artist." I knew he could play all the instruments, but I never actually auditioned him vocally. [*laughs*]

Here, I thought my perfect plan was solving all the problems, by not having to find a band and finding an artist who was good and played all the instruments. I thought my perfect plan had just gone belly-down, face-up, because I forgot to find out if he could actually sing the words, which was the reason I was doing this in the first place. [*laughs*] I was committed to finding a solution to that problem. If this had been an audition, and if I'd actually auditioned him beforehand, he would've failed the audition. But because I was already down the road with him, I had to find a way to make it work. We went back and forth and back and forth for hours in the studio, and nothing I could do or say would get him to sing any louder. It just wasn't happening. The longer we went, the worse it was getting, in terms of him feeling bad and intimidated and frustrated and shy. It wasn't going in the right direction. I was thinking, "I've got to come up with a little miracle here; because, otherwise, everything ends right here and now, and it's all the way back to the drawing board. I got an artist that I think I can work with. We're developing music and we're doing stuff together, and I'm liking what's happening, but the only problem is, I just can't get him to sing.

So we took a break, and I was really wracking my brain: "What can I do? What can I do? What can I do?" And finally, I came up with the idea of making a bed in the middle of the studio. I slept downstairs in the basement of my recording studio. I went downstairs and got my blankets and my pillows. I came upstairs and made a bed in the middle of the recording studio. I said, "Come over here. Lay down. I'm going to put a blanket on you. I want you to put your head on the pillow. I want you to get really relaxed." He said, "Well, why are you doing this? Why you doing it?" I said, "Don't worry about it. Just go with it."

I put him down, and I literally put him to bed in this self-made bed in the recording studio. Then, I turned off all the lights in the studio. I took my most sensitive microphone, and I put it as close to his mouth as I could. I said, "Look, you're all tucked in. You're all safe. You're all warm. The lights are off. I just want you to close your eyes. Just relax. I want you to imagine you're in your room by yourself at night at home, and you're just singing a song out loud and no one's around and no one can hear you." Over the course of some time, I eventually coaxed the voice out of him.

How many hours did that take?

Moon: It took all day. I didn't make him. I didn't create him. But, in that day, for the first time, I think he found his voice. It was always there. To sing, you've got to expose yourself. You've got to let someone see your soul. His singing was in a falsetto voice. That's not a very manly thing if you're feeling like you're not very manly to begin with and you're a teenager. He was sixteen. In that session, we found his voice together. It was pretty shaky at first, but over time, he learned that it was okay to sing in the style he wanted to sing. He got support and encouragement for it, then I taught him overdubbing. You know what overdubbing is? That's where you sing with yourself. Then you get three or four or about ten tracks of your voice. When he heard that, he really liked it. Because if you overdub any voice enough times, it always sounds cool. I had him overdubbing fairly early just to try and build the confidence in the sound of his voice. He really grooved on that. So that was one of the bigger things that happened for him in the studio very, very early on. Of course, I would sit down and teach him how to record a couple tracks, then I'd take him into the studio and I'd show him how to mix them together, and how he could use equalization and reverb and panning and level. All of that had an effect on the sound. Over the course of the year, I really taught him how to record and produce, which he, of course, never had any opportunity to be exposed to before. Who's going to give you unlimited time in the recording studio and sit there and teach you how to do it all for nothing?

He had an intensive one-on-one course in recording, producing, mixing, and engineering, which became his hallmark. Because once he understood that he could control his art, through controlling the recording, producing, engineering, and mixing process, he never went back. He never went out and sought out other people to produce him. He got dialed in early and that was the ultimate way to be. Then what did he do? He built a house that was a recording studio. Lived in a recording studio and spent his whole life recording.

That was the second thing that was career changing for him. The third thing that happened was—I worked in an ad agency and it was the largest ad agency in Minneapolis. It was tenth or twelfth in the country at the time. It was a pretty big ad agency called Campbell Mithun, and they were doing a lot of work with major national clients. They were teaching them how to use color, words, name recognition, and create an identity. I was bringing that all back and then applying it to the fundamentals of packaging out Prince. The first thing that happened was, after doing a few songs with him, I came home from the studio one day, from the ad agency, and I said, "Okay, I've written your first hit song." He asked, "How do you know it's going to be a hit song?" I said, "You know how I know, it's because this song has been written and designed to promote you as an artist. Most people go out and write songs that they just feel and think. This is a song written and engineered to market you as an artist, with your primary marketing concept in place." But he didn't know anything about marketing concepts, identity, image, and all of that at sixteen years old.

I said, "Let me explain to you what I had to do to write this song. What I had to do is to think about how someone markets a five-feet four-inch-Afro-haired kid from the North Side of town into the music industry and make you huge." He was all perked up, saying, "Okay, how?" I said, "Well, I looked at it. It's all about demographics and identifying your target audience. After doing some research, the target audience for music is people who buy music for kids from ten to sixteen years old. Those are people who buy more of this music. They've got the money to spend on it. Once they become eighteen and they go out into the world, they got to pay cars and rent and all the other stuff. The audience that we're trying to appeal to here is twelve- to sixteen-year-old young people. I don't think that guys are going to really relate to you, but I think we can get girls to relate to you. The way we can get girls to relate to you is by writing songs that have a sexual double meaning. In songwriting, it's called the double entendre. I've been thinking about this, and I've written this song that has a double-entendre sexual undertone. I think this should be the marketing theme that we use to promote you, because I think that's a very strong emotion that you can lock into and tie into young people. It will give you an identity."

He said, "Okay, that's really cool. That's really cool. What's the song called?" I said, "The song is called 'Soft and Wet.'" That was his first hit song. He asked, "What's the double meaning?" I said, "Well, don't you know?" He said, "I get the sexual meaning." [*laughs*] "What's the double meaning?"

I said, "The double meaning is—I'll fast-forward five years. My mother heard this song, and she was a proper British woman. She heard 'Soft and Wet' played on the radio. She came up to me in front of my whole family at the dinner table. She said, 'Son, I heard your song on the radio. It's great, I really like it but what is "Soft and Wet?"'" Now, here I am, in front of my mother, who, like I said, is straight as an arrow, I said to her, 'Mother, it's about a kiss.'" [*laughs*]

I explained to Prince that it being about a kiss "was the defendable position. You could say things that are highly sexual but also have

this innocent side to it. It creates a very powerful marketing asset. Go with that. We need to have a name and we need to have a color. These things need to work together. Now, let's talk about the name."

He said, "Well, I know what my name is going to be." I said, "Well, I know what your name is going to be. Let's just make sure we're all on the same page. I'll go first—I think your name should be Prince." I'm sitting waiting for him to go, "Yes, of course, duh." He goes, "Listen, I will never, ever, use that name. Forget it, it won't work, I don't agree, no, no, no." Prince's real name was Prince Rogers Nelson. Now, coming from the ad agency, learning how your name impacts these things, I thought we had been given a gift. I said, "You got the King… but there's never been a Prince. What a great image to work with." I could see exactly how the package is wrapped around Prince. He said, "No, no, no, no, no, no." He was vehemently against it. In fact, it ended up being a three-month-long argument that nearly broke us up in terms of a writing team. It was the biggest disagreement we ever had. You're probably wondering, "What did he think his name should be?"

After he told me that he did not want to go by the name Prince and that it would never, ever happen, I said, "Okay, what name are you thinking about using?" I was just dying to hear this, because I didn't know where he would go after this. He said, "There's only one name I will ever go by." I said, "Okay, what is it?" He said, "I just want you to understand there's only one possibility here with my name that I will even consider." I said, "Okay, what is it?" He said, "I want to be known as Mr. Nelson."

Interesting.

Moon: After three months, I finally said to him, "Either we do it my way, or I'm not going to work with you anymore, because I cannot make a Mr. Nelson famous. God could not make Mr. Nelson famous. As a name, it doesn't work. If we're going to keep working together, and if I'm going to keep paying all the bills and cover all your time, it's going to be Prince." He didn't like that at all. I mean, this was not a happy day between us, but I guess he didn't have a choice.

After we settled on "Prince," I said, "Now we need a color." I said, "Prince is royalty, so there is only one color we can choose. It's got to be purple." Because purple is the color of royalty. He agreed with that, and we had no problem on that topic. That's really how his image was developed and constructed over the course of the year that we worked together, and how the concept of sexual innuendo in his lyrics was developed and came out in his first hit song.

I had no idea.

Moon: Most people don't. I don't know what most people think. I think they think he had all these ideas and worked in the studio and said this is how we're going to do it, but it didn't happen that way at all. I've never heard anyone at any time report it that way. But this is one hundred percent accurate in terms of how it developed and why it developed the way it did. If you look back at it, it's really a lucky set of chances, really, that all lined up together. That's why I said, I think he was already born in the studio over that year, because, by the time he walked out, I wrote three of the four songs on his demo tape. He had an identity. He had the name. He had the color. He had a marketing image to go with him.

And then I went and found his manager to help him manage his career, which was Owen Husney, who was someone I knew. He walked in as this shy guy and walked out as a packaged artist. Let me be clear: *I didn't make him.* It was just—if we hadn't come together, what happened wouldn't have happened. He had the talent. It was just [that] somebody needed to bring it out of him. He needed the opportunity. It makes you wonder how many other kids in the inner city have all the talent in the world they need to be world-famous superstars but just never get the opportunity.

When you began working with him as a solo artist, where would you guys be positioned in your studio? Would he be working side by side with you?

Moon: We'd sit on the piano bench together. I have a pretty pitchy singing voice, but I feel a lot of melody in my head. So, we'd sit on piano together. He'd play the music. He wrote the music, and I wrote the words. Together, we would work out the arrangement for them. After we'd done three songs on his demo tape—we did maybe fifteen songs altogether, but it occurred to me that I was taking him in the direction that wasn't going to serve him long-term. He needed to be able to do this himself. So I told him, "For your demo tape, I want you to do one song that's all you. I want you to write the lyrics. I want you to produce it, mix it, do the music, and do it all without anything to do with me, because you need to know that you can also do this without me. You don't need to be dependent on me to get your artistic expression out." So the fourth song on his demo tape was a song that he had all done himself called "Baby."

What equipment and instruments did you have at your studio?

Moon: Well, back then, we did all of these songs on an eight-track, reel-to-reel cassette TASCAM recorder. I didn't have a lot of money. I built my recording studio from the money of selling vacuum cleaners. [*laughs*] It was scraped together with nickels and pennies here and there. So it wasn't the world's best equipment, but both of us came to it with more passion than the money, for sure. So one of the things that we would do with the studio was, we would experiment—I always told Prince I really wanted to experiment a lot. The Beatles had made a big impression on me. We used to do things backwards where the tape was playing backwards. We'd make sounds with pots and pans and singing through vacuum-cleaner hoses. We were swinging them and doing all kinds of singing into a Leslie organ speaker. We were doing all kinds of weird things. At the time, we were using [Shure] SM58s. We were using AKG C414s for vocal mics and Sony condensers. Then I had some UREI compressors in the studio. I had a guy build me a phaser/flanger. It was pretty good.

We had that built into the rack and it wasn't the most expensive equipment, but we used to do a lot of multitracking. So we'd do three voices, then mix it down to one, and then do another two voices and mix it down to one, and then mix those two down to one, and then to stack up our voices, because we only had eight tracks to work with. We were always having to bounce things around like crazy. So, that was the studio environment. And then, we would really spend all our free time in there every day or weekends. He'd always get so upset when I broke away to do anything other than work with him and spend time with him.

After he became famous, he called me up. This was three or four years later. He called me up out of the blue, and I said, "Hey, Prince. I haven't heard from you in a long time." He asked, "How are you doing? I'm so lonely. You know, I never realized, but when you're famous, you don't know why people are with you. Everyone wants to be with me. Everyone wants to be my friend. I know they just want me for my money and my fame. I feel so lonely because I can't really trust any connections that I've got with anybody. The only person that ever did anything for me, without really wanting anything back, was

you." What I heard in that phone call was the same young sixteen-year-old, kind-of-scared kid trying to sing in my studio, now out in the world, famous with all the money, still realizing that he was still scared. It was still a lonely world, even though he was achieving his dream and getting everything he wanted in life, but it really wasn't the end all to everything that it could have been. In fact, I did an interview recently with the BBC. The BBC asked me a question that was interesting. They asked, "How do you feel about having discovered Prince and your work with him?" After he died, I really asked myself that question, and I'm not sure that I really did him a favor. I think, if I had to go back and do it all over again, I might not have discovered him. I might not have taken him where I took him. And maybe he would have had a really ordinary life, and married a really ordinary girl, and had a really ordinary family, and lived a really ordinary life and been happier.

My deal with Prince from the beginning was the fact that I was going to do whatever I could to make him famous. There was only one thing I wanted. He asked, "What's that?" I said, "The only thing I want is that any songs we write together, you give me credit for my songs. My only reason for doing this is, I just love music. I'd like to see you get out there, and I'd like to see you get out there with at least one of my songs." People say, "Wow, if you could go back and do it again, don't you wish you got him under contract? Or don't you wish you got a bigger piece of him?" I say, "No, because I got all done packaging him up, and we finished his demo tape." He came to me and said, "I want you to be my manager." I said, "No way. I had no interest in being a manager. I do this because I love music. I'm not interested in booking your hotels, making sure you get on the plane, and seeing if you got food in your room. That doesn't interest me at all. I'll find someone to do that, but I won't be a manager. It's not a job I'm interested in." I found him a good manager. I did the piece with him I wanted him to do.

How did you bring him to Owen Husney?

Moon: Owen was managing another artist; it was a folk artist who was recording in the studio at that time. So Owen would come over to the studio sometimes, and sit with me, while we were recording, and he was working with these real prim and proper couple of White guys singing folk songs. But he was a solid manager. He was a good businessman. He had a little ad agency, and he had the understanding of the ad agency background and the marketing components I had put into Prince that he had to leverage them into the next step. When I was thinking about trying to find his manager for him, Owen came to mind fairly quickly because I knew him. Even though I was a recording engineer/producer/writer, I was really a marketing person first. All my life, I've been doing marketing, so that was always a passion of mine. Owen was a natural person to pass the baton to. I'll never forget the line that I used that day. I said, "Owen, I've got the next Stevie Wonder. He can play all the instruments. He's sixteen years old, but he's not blind." That was my pitch. I played this four-song demo that I had written and produced with Prince. He said, "Okay. It's not bad. Let me listen to it." I kept coming back for the rest of the week, every day, saying, "Owen, have you spent more time? Have you listened to the tape?"

Then after about a week, he came and said, "You know, okay, I'm hearing it. I think you got something here." I think what he did was he went off and played it for other people and started getting some good feedback. Then he said, "Yes, I think you got something here. I'd like to work with your artist." I said, "I'm not looking for anything. I'll hand him off to you. The only deal is the same deal I did with Prince. Anything that comes out that I wrote, I want to make sure it's got my name on it." Owen took it from there and got him a deal with Warner Bros.

Artist: Prince
Album: *For You*
Label: Warner Bros.
Release year: 1978
Produced, arranged, composed, and performed by: Prince
"Soft and Wet" lyrics co-written by: Chris Moon
Executive produced, engineered, and mixed by: Tommy Vicari
Recorded at: Record Plant (Sausalito, California)
Cover photo by: Joe Giannetti

How did you begin working with Prince?

Owen Husney: The first time I met him actually was when Chris Moon brought him over to my house. I had already heard the demo by that point. I was quite enamored with what I heard, but I still didn't know what he looked like or anything. Chris already told me that it wasn't a band. It was one kid playing everything, which was pretty unusual in those days, except for maybe Stevie Wonder. The fact that he was so young and he was doing it was cool. Actually, he didn't really want to meet at my office. We met over at my house; I was living in Minneapolis with my wife at that time. I was sort of thrilled to see that he was also cute. [*laughs*] I was in showbiz, so I was trying to figure out every aspect of it. I said to myself, "Please don't be that gifted *and* ugly or 475 pounds." [*laughs*] I was just praying, and I listened to the demo tape like six hundred times.

So, I was very prepared when he came over. I could tell that he was a very bright human being, even though he was that young. He was grasping a lot of different concepts. I was probably ten years older at that time. But I could tell that he was very bright, aside from the music, which was important to me. I could just tell by the way he was conducting himself, and by some of the questions that he was asking me, that there wasn't some bullshit going on there. He was grasping a lot of the things that I was throwing out at the time. I was asking him some questions. I was asking him about his influences. Because I was a musician myself, I had a lot of instruments around the house. He gravitated to the instruments and was still talking, which really made it nice because it broke the ice.

I listened to his demo a thousand times, and I was watching him, like I'm sure he was probably watching me at the time, and trying to figure each other out. I think there were some things that I threw out that he got right away, and we formed this little friendship. I've worked with many, many artists in my lifetime. Everybody is always leery when they meet a manager. I could see that he was leery and checking me out, but what he did or did not know that I was checking him out to see, "Hey, can I work with this dude? Is it a workable situation?" I had a saying that there are no superstars who are still living in their mother's basement who should have made it. You have to have talent and drive, and that's the most important thing. I knew he had the talent. I was checking him out to see, "Okay, is this going to be a drug situation?" Because I had been through that. "Is this going to be a kind of attitude situation?" Because I had been through that too. All these things were sabotage and killers to the artists, especially in the beginning. He didn't seem to have any of that.

He seemed to be very directed and focused. When I said something, he was listening. He wasn't, like, off in the corner looking at flowers or anything. He was there, he wanted know, and because of that, in that first meeting, I was very enthused to go to work with him and see what I could do. Again, you have to understand, at the beginning of an artist's career, it's fifty percent management and fifty percent artist. Once the artist starts to make it, they're generating money, and they're doing it, obviously, it becomes all about the artist at that point. And because he was so young, he needed me. I can tell that he needed me because I was a little bit older than him, and I had been around the block. He needed my information and my experience. We all know that Prince, at some point, became entirely his own boss, but it was not that way in the beginning; I knew this young vulnerable kid who came into my house. When I mourned his death, I mourned that kid that came to my house. There was a very young, vulnerable kid living in André Cymone's basement at that time.

Can you delve more into your first interaction with Prince? Did you guys just talk about music?

Husney: Yes. We talked about a lot of things, and I kind of have this sense of humor that some people just don't get and some people get, and he got it. Because I will just all of a sudden say something out of the blue that other people would be like, "Huh, what?" I know Chris [Moon] was doing that, because he was at the first meeting. There was a reason I did that. I could tell Chris was kind of like, "Huh?" But Prince got it, and he would laugh his ass off. I thought, okay, he has a sense of humor. He gets it. He gets what's going on. I had met a lot of people from other record labels at the time, and I had some near misses in management. I had an act that Columbia Records wanted to sign. But I met an attorney who I became friends with, until he was killed about two years ago [in a cycling accident]. He was a very famous attorney named Milt Olin, and he just looked at me one day, and he said, "You know what, Husney, you're one of us." And when I met Prince, that was the same feeling I had. It was like, "Hey, man, you're one of us. You get it. You get the bullshit, you understand this stuff." And that was very appealing to me. I could tell that he was pretty driven.

Take me back to the first time you heard his demo, and what songs were on that demo that you heard?

Husney: The demo was some stuff that he and Chris had done at Chris's Moon Sound Studios. Prince could come over to Chris's studio anytime he wanted to. So a lot of what I heard were very long songs, longer than you would want on a demo tape. But I could hear that there was some serious talent. I actually asked Chris what was the name of the band. He just looked at me and said, "Hey, it's one kid. He just turned eighteen, and he is singing and playing everything." I was like, "Okay. Let's go to the next stuff. Let's listen to that one too." I think one of the first things I heard was a song they had cowritten called "Soft and Wet," which was the first single. I didn't know where the impetus came from, because "Soft and Wet" was very suggestive at the time. I didn't know who came up with this layer and what was going on, but they had pretty much cowritten that song.

[The other songs] were good, but they were almost jam songs. They were very long. I was listening with a commercial ear all the time back then. I'd been through the mill, so I understood how some of those A&R guys thought. The whole time I was thinking, "Boy, if I ever get to manage this guy, these songs are going to have to be two minutes in length," which I knew wasn't going to make him happy, but I had to do it. Later on, I just started listening to everything that he was writing. We would sit and listen and get everything that he was writing. He trusted me at that time, because he was a kid, and I was the dude in town; but I think he respected the fact that I had come from the basis of being a musician, and I had my own little hit record myself ["(Turn on Your) Love Light" by the High Spirits]. I think that gave him a lot of confidence. I didn't think anybody else had all of that going for them, and he was smart enough to recognize that.

Now, when he started working with you, was he still living with André, or did he move in with you?

Husney: Yes, he was still living with André, but he was spending a lot of time in my house at that point and with André. These guys were like glue. They were always jamming together. They could sort of read each other's mind. André was a very gifted guy. I was over at his house and saw the famous basement. I began to gather that André

*"All of this and more is for you.
With love, sincerity and
deepest care, my life with you
I share."**

SIDE ONE   BSK 3150

For You
Prince: All vocals

In Love
*Prince: All lead and background vocals, guitars, Orr bass,
Ms. Poly Moog, syndrums, Arp Pro Soloist, Arp String Ensemble*

Soft and Wet
*Prince: All lead and background vocals, synthesizer bass,
singing bass, drums, guitars, clavinet, Ms. Poly Moog, Oberheim
4-voice, Arp Soloist, slapsticks*

Crazy You
*Prince: Vocals, acoustic guitar, Finga cymbals, wind chimes,
congas, electric guitars, water drums*

Just as Long as We're Together
*Prince: All lead and background vocals, guitars, Orr bass,
drums, bongos, Fender Rhodes piano, clavinet, Mini-moog,
Fuzz bazz, Arp String Ensemble, Arp Soloist,
Handclapsandfingasnaps*

THE OTHER SIDE
Baby
*Prince: All lead and background vocals, acoustic guitar, Orr bass,
electric guitars, acoustic piano, Oberheim 4-voice, Arp Soloist,
orchestra bells, Fender Rhodes piano, Mini-moog, drums*

My Love Is Forever
*Prince: All lead and background vocals, Fender Rhodes piano,
guitars, Orr bass, woodblocks, Ms. Poly Moog, drums, Oberheim
4-voice, Arp Pro Soloist, guitar solo*

So Blue
*Prince: Vocals, brush trap, Orr bass, electric guitar,
acoustic guitar, tree bell, bass solo*

I'm Yours
*Prince: All vocals, electric guitars, Orr bass, drums, clavinet,
acoustic guitar, syndrums, bass and guitar solos*

---

*Special thanks to God, Owen, Britt, Bernadette, My Father and
Mother, Russ Thyret, Gary, David Rivkin/Sound 80 Studios,
C. Moon, Eddie, Sharon and Eleanor, L. Phillips, Bobby "Z"
Rivkin, Tom Coster, Graham Lear, Joe Giannetti, Patrice Rushen,
Charles Veal, Jr., Shirley Walker, Knut Koupeé Music,
Chuck Orr, Lisa H., and You!*

For You inner sleeve with credits, showing Prince's mastery of instruments at such a young age.

was a very integral part of it. Both of them hung out over at my house all the time, because I had an office and I had an ad agency; I was gone during the day. So Prince was free to come into my house. I had a tape recorder that you could bounce tracks internally on. He used that as he would record and hang out. Then we began to have countless dinners together. It was really funny, because when we went to do the first album in Sausalito at the Record Plant [in 1977], André was there. He was telling my son this at the First Avenue [club] last August; I overheard him. André told him when he and Prince met me and [my son's] mom, who's now my ex-wife, it was the first sense of family that either of them ever had. And André said, "And it was White people." [*laughs*] It was the first time they ever ate salad before dinner. André said, "The brothers on the North Side weren't eating salad." It was interesting to hear André's take on it, but I guess it was true that we were kind of a family. We had become kind of a family. Prince trusted my wife and me, and we really loved him. He was a very cool guy. We just wanted to make sure that he made it.

Please talk about your move out to the West Coast to record?

Husney: Yes, that was very interesting because I did the demo tapes. I knew I couldn't make a deal on the Moon Sound demos. They were just eight-track recordings. The quality wasn't good enough, and the songs were way too long. I had another bandmate of mine, David Rivkin. David Z is what he goes by today. He got into engineering and recording acts. As a matter of fact, David is probably really one of the forefathers, because he staked his claim recording the young, Black musicians and bands in Minneapolis, well before Prince. David and I were in competing bands in our youths. Then he joined my band, and we toured for a long time. In my mind, there was only one person who could do the demos and that was David. We recorded in Minneapolis at Sound 80 [Studios]. I only wanted three, really well done demos. Then, I left to go out to California. I was lying my way into the record labels and pitching them. Eventually, I got a deal with Warner Bros. We wanted to always record in Minneapolis, so I cut a deal with the studio because it was a state-of-the-art room. Minneapolis was a real hotbed of music. People didn't even know that. We definitely had talent there for a long time. It was a big commercial area, too, for ad agencies. This was an up-to-the-minute, contemporary, state-of-the-art studio.

Were you in those sessions with David Z?

Husney: Yes. I was there all the time. I put them together. I put everybody there. I brought everybody and put them together.

When they were working on those tracks, what was their interaction like in the studio?

Husney: David was a consummate musician, and he really knew his way around recording. David also had perfect pitch. So I knew that Prince had no problems with David. David worked with Prince all the way through *Purple Rain* and…afterward. Prince really liked him. I don't ever remember Prince coming to me and saying, "Whoa, this David guy, get him out of here." Never. I don't remember them having a problem. I think they were the perfect match. When it came to vocals, David had perfect pitch, but he also knew that when harmonies are off, and especially when one person's doing all of the harmony parts like Prince was doing, when they're just a little bit off, that's where you get a richness of sound. When harmonies are dead on, it's sterile. David understood that. They were the perfect match, which

is why I was heartbroken when Warner Bros. wanted someone who had more gold and platinum than David did on the wall. Ironically, when we went to record the first album, David went into the studio with another group, [Lipps, Inc., whose leader Steven Greenberg] was literally playing bar mitzvahs and weddings. This guy had an idea for a song and he brought it to David, and David completely retooled that song and brought in every snare sound and every sound and it became a number one hit. This was while we were doing the first album. Every free country in the world knows the song called "Funkytown." So David was very instrumental in helping us from a recording and sound point of view to get that deal. Obviously, Prince had his own mind. He knew the direction, and David knew how to work with him in that direction in the studio.

During the recording process of making the demo with Mr. Rivkin and Prince, where would they be positioned in the studio?

Husney: I have pictures of them, but I can't share them with you. I have pictures of our very first night. David would be at the console and Prince would be next to him. It was really the same with Chris Moon and Prince. They were sitting right there side by side.

What was his typical studio routine? Would Prince come in and work with him at a certain time?

Husney: Yes, because I had set up so many hours that would be enough time for them. It was nonstop even back then. I mean, that's what Prince was put on Earth to do. That was it. And so I would be recording him at my office. I eventually got a studio together there, but I had an office with twenty employees because I owned an ad agency. They would leave at six o'clock, and then they'd come back to the studio. We'd push the desks off to the side, and then we would just jam until all hours in the morning. So even though the studio might have been a little bit more structured at that time because we didn't own it, the music did not stop.

Why wasn't the debut album recorded there?

Two things happened: Warner Bros. thought that David was too new, which I thought was a mistake. I had to represent Prince and tell the chairman of Warner Bros. that an eighteen-year-old kid that had never made an album before was also going to produce his own album. So we negotiated a deal, and Warner Bros. said, "Okay, we'll give it to Prince, but we'll need an engineer who's already got gold and platinum on his walls. You can either do it in L.A., or we will fly that engineer into Minneapolis." I was heartbroken because I wanted David Z to do it. Because I knew how talented he was, and I knew that he really got along, in a musical sense, with Prince. There was just no doubt about it. But they insisted—Prince knew that we couldn't push the envelope. We got him to become his own producer. We couldn't push it too far, so we agreed to have an engineer come in, [Tommy Vicari], and he had [a lot of] experience.

The original plan was to begin recording…at Sound 80 Studios in Minneapolis, Minnesota. Vicari and Prince were going to work at that studio for two months on his debut album. Vicari was going to fly in for two months and serve as executive producer, because the deal that was made with Warner Bros. was that Prince would serve as main producer, but the execs at Warner Bros. wanted a seasoned, veteran producer to serve as the executive producer on the album. The studio got so excited that they decided to put in a new recording console.

That's a no-no in this business. I owned three studios in my lifetime, and that's a real no-no. It usually took a month or two to get a board under control once you wired it in. Vicari said he couldn't work in that studio, so he wanted to go back to Los Angeles to record. Tommy Vicari was from L.A. and felt more comfortable out there.

I made the decision that I did not want to go to Los Angeles with Prince. I knew who he was, and I knew how he liked to operate. I compromised and said, "Okay, we'll leave the studio in Minneapolis." Prince was a Minneapolis guy and didn't want to go, but I talked him into it, and we compromised on the Record Plant in Sausalito, California, where Sly [Stone] did quite a bit of his work there. It was a very good room. They agreed to it, and I went out and found us a house in Marin County. We flew out there. The whole family: my then wife, André, Prince, me, and my dog. [laughs] We all went out as one happy family living in Sausalito.

You have to remember: Prince and André had probably very limited travel experiences at that time. And here they are—Marin County is one of the most expensive real estate areas in the world. We were out there living in a three-level redwood home that I swung for us. It wasn't too far from Sausalito. I could drive Prince because he didn't have a driver's license or car at that time. I was the designated driver that drove everybody around. My wife was making dinners and helping Prince with his hair. We were turning him on to other forms of music like Joni Mitchell. André was there as well. André was really Prince's soul-mate companion during that first process.

There were a lot of great stories when we were recording. We would take a break for a day, because it was getting intense. One of the things they loved to do was to have me drive them into San Francisco. They would just go to some music store there and jam like crazy. I would drop them off, and they would jam there with all the instruments. One day, I got a call from this dude, and he said, "Hey, man. I saw these two dudes jamming at the music store in San Francisco. We want to come over to the house." I was like, "No, I don't want anybody out at the house. This is ridiculous. They're working, we can't do it." I said, "Who are you?" He said, "We're in Santana's band. Carlos saw them jamming, and he went crazy over them. We want to come out to the house and hang with you guys." I was like, "Oh shit." [laughs] So, here are these two guys from over north in Minneapolis, who are now—Prince hasn't even made his first album—influencing the big musicians at that time like Santana, just from jamming in a music store. That was the enormity of his talent. I was a guitar player. When I was living in Minneapolis, if I sat for ten years in my basement playing guitar, I would've never been as good as Prince's natural talent. Either you're born that way or you're not.

So it was a really good experience. André was there. Prince had an ability to absorb a lot of stuff. The engineer [Tommy Vicari] was great. I mean, he had a huge track record. But Prince didn't want anybody dictating any kind of musical direction to him. After a while, he said, "Owen, I can do most of this myself. Can you let the engineer go?" And I didn't want to let him go because he was a good guy. Then I knew I would have record-label problems; but again, I have to give Warner Bros. credit. They really understood Prince. Warner Bros. gave him everything that he wanted: all the tools and the keys to the kingdom. They understood him. They got him. They got who he was as an artist. That's why I wanted to be there, because they were a very artist-friendly record label. Mo Ostin was the chairman, Lenny Waronker was the president, and Russ Thyret was head of promotions; they all would have fallen on a sword for Prince, because they believed in him as much as I did.

Were there major differences between the Record Plant and Sound 80 Studios?

Husney: Yes, Sound 80 was a little bit more sterile and you probably would expect to see more white lab coats there. [laughs] The Record Plant in Sausalito, California, was a very funky, wooden studio known for just great sound with a giant tongue in one of the studios, a lounge chair in the shape of an elevated tongue, and that's where Sly would record. He could plug into the tongue and stuff like that and just record or sing right from there. All those places were still holdovers from the hippie days with everything being natural. But it wasn't as sterile as Sound 80. It was funkier. It was a good room to make that first record in. They had a little FM transmitter, so we could do a mix or just do a rough cut, and then get in our car and drive around about a nine-block radius, then listen to it on the radio and see how it would sound, which actually worked. Because you have to remember, we were in a big, giant, million-dollar studio, and basically, at that time, we were cutting records that were coming out of tiny speakers. We had to be very aware of how that sound was going to translate. But it was a very funky room, really cool place, very typical San Francisco-ish, hippie-vibe-ish, Sly Stone situation. It really turned out to be good.

How much time was spent at the Record Plant recording the songs for the album For You?

Husney: It seemed like day and night. I kept pushing the boundaries of Warner Bros.' budget. In all the books, it says, "They went way over budget." Considering the artist that he became, it really was meaningless. I pushed Warner Bros. I pushed them like crazy. We needed extra time. I think retrospectively, and I'm sure Prince would say the same thing, that he probably tried to be too perfect on that first album. He knew it was his debut. I think that he tried to go over it again and again and to make it a perfect album, which he was capable of doing. If you were to ask him, he'd say, "Yes, I probably put too much time in. I didn't give it enough air to breathe. I probably overdid it." But they were going all the time. Prince really liked recording at night, so that's what musicians do and that's what he did. I'd drop him off at night at the studio. They'd work all night. He'd come home early in the morning. But he was working around the clock. We had it on lockout, which meant they locked out the room for us, so it was our room.

For the nine songs that are on the record, were you there during the collaboration process between Prince and the engineer, Tommy Vicari?

Husney: Yes. Look, I'm sensitive enough. I was a musician, and I wouldn't want my manager sitting in the studio all day long. There was no reason for me to do that because I had to be up during the day to be dealing with the record label and working off promotional programs and promotional tours. It didn't make much sense for me to be a studio hanger-on. I don't even like doing it to this day, although I'm semi-retired. I'm not out to make anybody self-conscious, but I did see the process. Trust me, I heard the problems that would happen, especially when Prince and the engineer fell out. It wasn't because the engineer wasn't good. It was because Prince had an ability to learn at such a rapid rate. Prince didn't come home and say, "Wow, I learned how to EQ something today." No. Prince would come home and say, "I've learned how everything works." *Everything*. It was more than amazing to watch. He was a sponge—he was SpongeBob on twelve. He just pulled everything in. It was nothing personal for anybody that

he worked with, but as soon as he started to fully understand it, it was time for him to do it himself. I've never seen that with anybody I've worked with. People know their way around now because it's digital, but back then it was a pretty interesting process. You were still editing tape by cutting it. He understood everything from A to Z, and it was very awesome to watch.

What was some of the equipment and the instruments that were used during the creative process?

Husney: He was very enamored with synthesizers. Actually, we talked about it at one point, the usage of synthesizers. In the very beginning, it was just another creative tool, so I was able to get him one—it was an Oberheim Four Voice synthesizer. He grasped how it worked, immediately. He used it on some of the horn parts, especially on the demos at Sound 80 [Studios]. The only person I know that actually did some stuff with him that came out during the first album was Patrice Rushen. She showed him a bunch of stuff, and he did some stuff with her. Otherwise, he did it by himself. He was very enamored with the early Oberheim Four Voice synthesizer. He continued to use it quite a bit. That became part of the Minneapolis sound. Other people overused it to the point where it was totally overdone. He knew how to layer it. He was laying down the drum tracks, guitar, and bass. He was laying it all down and putting it together. His use of the synthesizer was the biggest standout that I remember at the time. It really was influencing his sound.

How much was Prince involved with engineering *For You*?

Husney: I think that's where some of the dispute came in, because Prince had a very specific way that he wanted his music to sound early on. He had two things going for him: he had the talent to pull it off, and he had the balls to pull it off. He would go for it, and if you got in his way, it wasn't going to work out too well for you, even at an early age. In fact, one of the things I noticed about Prince that I liked early on was he knew what he wanted and he had the balls to go for it. I never saw him back down. [*laughs*] That kind of talent doesn't come along very often. A lot of people do have it, but very few [overall].

Were there any interesting, behind-the-scenes stories in terms of the making of the couple of songs that were released from the record, like "Soft and Wet," "Just as Long as We're Together," "For You"?

Husney: On "For You," I don't know where he dreamt that up. Somewhere on the plane going out there or sometime in the studio. He just kind of came up with that. The only thing that I can tell you is that we were all thrown into this situation in Sausalito, and we had to make the best of it. One of the things that kept us going was, we were constantly doing practical jokes on people. At one point, Prince wanted David [flown] out during the vocals, because he really trusted David. So I flew David out to Sausalito, and he stayed with us and did a lot of the vocals. Prince always trusted David on vocals. But, I think, David was even shocked by the amount of practical jokes we were pulling on each other. We would go to a restaurant, and Prince would have a squirt gun. From under the table, he fired it up in the air; it would be landing on different peoples' heads. [*laughs*] They were like, "What the hell is going on?" People would be brushing their shoulders off all over the restaurant. We pulled all kinds of practical jokes. It helped to break the ice. He was definitely a leader in the practical-joke department.

Did you have a favorite song on this album?

Husney: Yes, I did. There was a song on the first album called "In Love." No, "So Blue." I mean, "So Blue." "In Love" I liked, because when he hit it, that was a synthesizer arrangement. It was very hard to get out of my mind. There was a song called "So Blue" on that first album, which really showed the tender side of Prince. It showed how multifaceted he was. There were probably several personalities swimming around in there. There was that "So Blue" side, which was the spirited, vulnerable person. One of the songs that really stood out to me, because it was on the demo, was a song called "Baby." "Baby, what are we gonna do?" It was about young teenagers getting pregnant. They were dating and his girlfriend got pregnant. "Baby, what are we gonna do? There's [barely] enough money for two." Where are you going to go with that? At the very end of the song, he says, "I hope our baby has eyes just like yours." He wasn't talking about abortion or anything. It was very, very sensitive for an eighteen-year-old to be writing that shit. He could see all sides of everything. He was so bright. It was just like I said before—people like him don't come along very often. ◗

ANDRÉ CYMONE talks about his newest album
and reminisces about the early, lost recordings by Prince and company.

THE REBEL

by Ericka Blount Danois

The day that Prince died, childhood friend, bandmate, and family member André Cymone was going into the studio in New York to mix the last song for his new album, *1969*.

"I called my engineer," Cymone remembers. "I couldn't do it."

If there's any musician that knows Prince, it would be Cymone, who had lived with Prince as a brother-from-another-mother in Cymone's mother's basement when they were kids before the creation of their first band, Grand Central, and later serving as an integral part—songwriting, producing, and musicianship—on Prince's early albums before going solo.

"When I got back home, I ended up finishing that song. My son helped me come up with a beat," Cymone says. "I think my son cried more than anyone I've seen cry since Prince died."

We are living in crazy times, and for some, the prevailing thought is that Prince checked out, along with many of our icons—Muhammad Ali, David Bowie—before they had to witness it. Cymone's newest album, *1969*, examines social injustice, civil rights, and racism, without being didactic. It is a consciously rebellious rock album that allows for levity amidst the mayhem.

"With all the stuff that's going on right now, it's like we are reliving 1969 all over again," Cymone says by phone. "This is Groundhog Day."

Cymone talks about reliving the past, but his album is far less a walk through nostalgia than it is a testament to a time when, as Slick Rick says, "people wore pajamas and lived life slow." Cymone takes his time to produce timeless work—whether it's a band member using a Fender Rhodes instead of an electronic keyboard, or playing all of the instruments himself. It's the craft that's nostalgic, not the work.

Wax Poetics spoke with André Cymone about Prince, the new album, the Rebels project, and everything in between.

Who did you work with, and what led you to *1969*?

I used the same backing band, but I decided to do all the leads—lead guitar and rhythm and bass on a handful of songs.

When I was a kid in 1969, I liked all kinds of music—rock, Motown, James Brown, and funk. I thought if I could make an album with all these different music influences—the Monkees, the Beatles, the Byrds, songs like [the Lemon Pipers'] "Green Tambourine"—I could create almost like a time machine. You should be able to go back and re-create a time period, because time is just a frame of mind. If I could put myself in that time period and go back and create, I would create this album.

Who inspired the first track, "We All Need Somethin'"?

I would say Sly. If Rolling Stones, Jimi Hendrix, and Sly had a baby, it would be that song. Jimi was definitely a big influence for this record.

Tell me about "California Way"—what was the inspiration behind it?

I had gone to Malibu with my family, we drove to the beach, and that's when that song kind of popped into my head. My daughter was out here. It was just beautiful, just one of those days.

Me and my ten-year-old came up with the beat. The concept for that particular song came from the day I went to the Prince memorial on Wilshire. On my way there, I kept him humming "do do do." I was talking to [former bandmates] Dez [Dickerson], talking to Bobby [Z]. I kept humming it and my son helped me come up with the beat.

You decided to put out the EP, *Black Man in America*, first.

Yes, those songs on the EP are speaking to where we are right now. "Hot Night in the Neighborhood" isn't on the [new] album and that's something I wrote right after Mike Brown died [after being shot multiple times by a police officer in Ferguson, Missouri, in 2014]. "Hallelujah" is a song that's, hopefully, the bridge, the redemption where we can get past all of this and get to the other side. Those two [songs] aren't on the [new] album.

Were you able to reunite with the family for the Prince tribute?

I agreed to do their tribute first. Then the Revolution asked me to do theirs. They said we are going to do ours before the family. I thought that was interesting, so I said, "Let me ask the family." I wanted to make sure they didn't have a problem with it. They didn't, so I did it. They originally had two shows and they sold out in ninety seconds. I originally wanted to do just a couple of songs, and I ended up doing eight.

Tell me how the July 1979 sessions known as the Rebels project came to be.

I think the concept came about just to keep us busy. We had just come off tour and people get antsy and start getting involved in other things if you don't find something for them to do.

Our first tour Prince lost his voice in Philadelphia, so we put off the Rebels project. We had to go right back out, and after we came off that tour, he was going to make the *Dirty Mind* album. I think, somewhere in between, there was the Rebels project. Dez did a lot of writing. I did a lot of writing, but I think some of the

other guys were getting kind of restless. Prince was like, "Let's see what happens if we do something with the band." So we called ourselves the Rebels and we went out to Boulder, Colorado, to record.

We did rock-climbing. We went out on the local college scene. We got to know each other. I got to know those guys a lot better because we were stuck in a weird place. I didn't take it seriously. We took a gang of pictures. Me and Dez and Gayle [Chapman] did the [Rebels'] "You" song hanging out by the swimming pool. We were maybe nineteen, twenty years old.

We did a whole album's worth of material. I don't think it was ever meant to be released. I think it just gave us something to do.

Was it the label that didn't want it to be released?

It was either Prince, his management, or the label that didn't want it released. We never knew anything.

Some of the songs, like "If I Luv U 2 Nite," which Mica Paris recorded, ended up being produced by other artists. Prince's version is more of a ballad.

"U" went to Paula Abdul [which was produced by Prince as "Paisley Park"], which was Gayle's song, but Prince wrote most of it. I know the record company wanted the song I did to be a single, "Thrill You or Kill You." Dez had what I thought was the coolest song on the whole project, which was "Disco Away." Disco was still really an issue back then, and Dez was such a rock-and-roll dude with a passion. It was a play on words—"Disco Away"—"leave me alone, I want to rock-and-roll." It was a funny song.

"Thrill You or Kill You" was kind of funky with a weird disco beat. I still have the original cassette with all the tracks on it. On the cassette, there's "Let's Work" when it was called "Let's Rock." I have a bunch of stuff we did that was never released.

How did the Prince tribute go?

During the show, I had a bad moment. Morris [Day] showed up to open up the show and I hadn't talked to Morris in a long time. We went through the whole catching-up thing. I was saying it really hadn't hit me yet. We know Prince and we know him well. If there was anybody to fake this situation, [we joked] it would be him, and we started laughing. He was like, "You go back with Prince even before me." That stuck in my head. I went out and did the first couple of songs, I think "Uptown," and I kept thinking about what he said. I was sitting there and, all of a sudden, it hit me. When you think about Prince, he's had so many reinventions and what finally hit me is that I went back to the dude that I knew when we were kids and I realized that dude is gone. He's gone. I'm standing up there and tears just start coming out of my eyes. I said, "I gotta get my shit together." I saw [singer] Kip Blackshire, who was on the show as well, and he was like, "I think you're supposed to be out there right now." I was like, "What?" He was like, "Yeah." I was like, "Oh shit!" They were doing ["The Ballad of] Dorothy Parker." All of a sudden, I could hear them playing it. They were doing a flute solo. I

started singing, "Dorothy was a waitress..." It was really beautiful. It was a blessing to see that he had such amazing people, spiritually good people around him.

In so many ways, it's unbelievable. We said so many times [to each other], "We gotta hook up," and you always think you have time. We were talking about "it's a shame" and "we shouldn't let so much time go by." You think you have time. I keep trying to find scenarios where it's not real. ◗

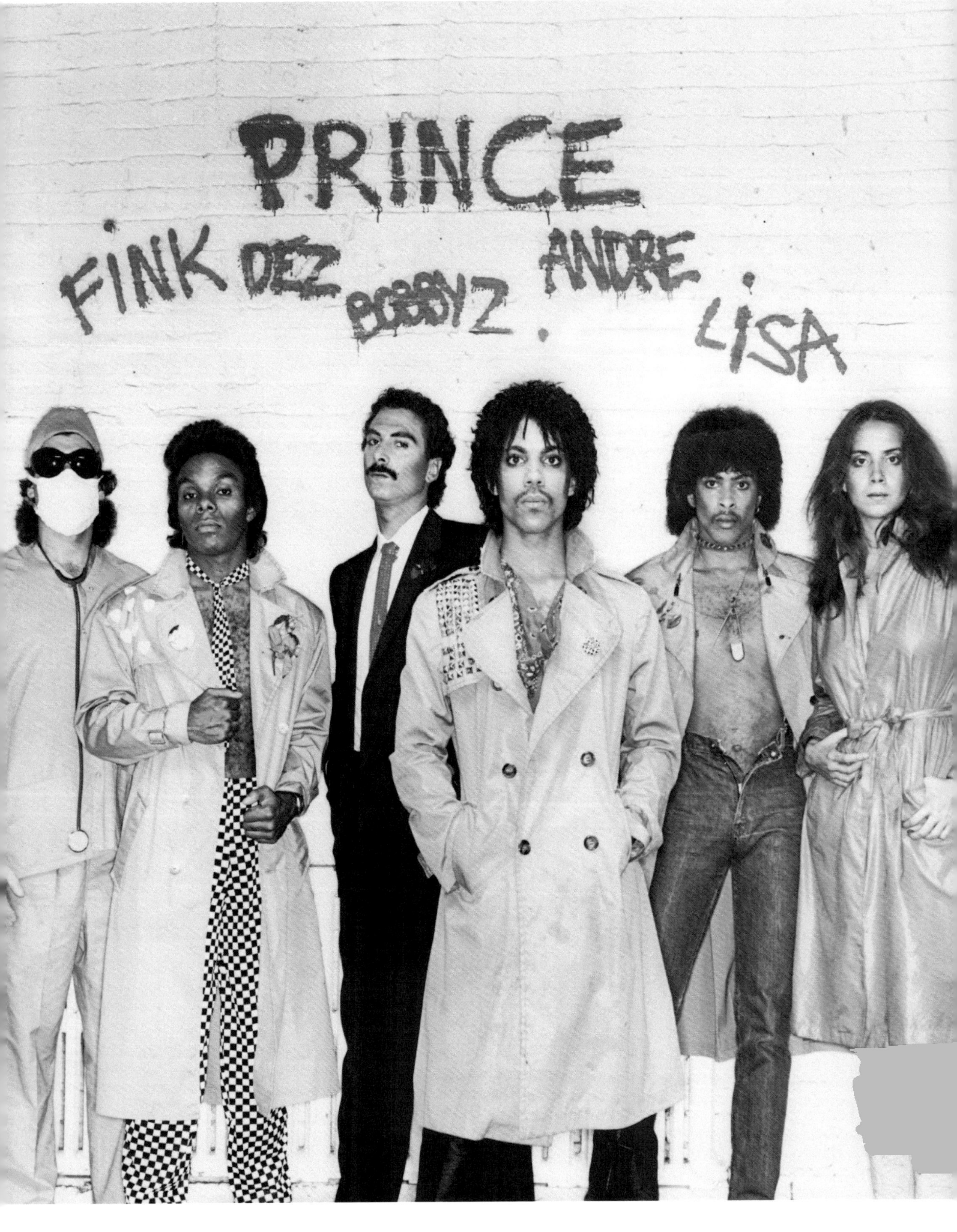
PRINCE
FINK
DEZ
BOBBY Z
ANDRE
LISA

After two self-contained albums, Prince started gigging with a band who would support him on 1980's *Dirty Mind*. After a couple lineup changes, including the departure of his childhood friend André Cymone, the new band stabilized with keyboardist Doctor Fink, drummer Bobby Z., bassist Brown Mark, and guitarist and pianist duo Wendy and Lisa. Prince would find his musical soul mates in this new group, dubbed THE REVOLUTION, who would join him on an extraordinary run of hit albums that would leave the world a better place.

AGENTS OF CHANGE

by A. D. Amorosi

One of the strangest aspects regarding 2016's loss of Prince and David Bowie—innovative artists who moved modern music forward in their own individualistic fashion—was speaking with those who aided each in making their densest, most formidable recordings.

With Bowie, it was his first, last, and most consistent studio producer, Tony Visconti; his *Let's Dance* collaborator Nile Rodgers; his guitarist-arranger Carlos Alomar who helped bring the singer from glam to soul then electronica; and the impressionist saxophonist that steered Bowie to a grand *Blackstar* finale, Donny McCaslin. To a man, they heralded Bowie's genius, while taking little credit themselves for their master's voice, no matter how integral each musician or technician's contribution was to the main-man's canon. Bowie's work, however, changed so radically from album to album that its finest players got lost in the stars. Bowie's Spiders from Mars dressed like their otherworldly front man, but you never got the feeling they too were sexually alternative aliens like Ziggy Stardust.

Prince worked his paisley palate of funky soul-sonic psychedelia like a dog gnawing a bone, and most of his incredible players were happily faceless within that swirl.

Not Prince's the Revolution.

To say they were radically different—operating wildly apart from how any other bandleader and backing band might interact—is an understatement. If he was loud, they were louder. If he was strong, they were stronger. If he was funky, they were funkier. If he was sexy, they were sexier. They had to be. No one will ever say any of that of Prince's band from *Rave Un2 the Joy Fantastic*.

Referring to the Revolution, keyboardist Matt "Doctor" Fink jokes, "I'd like to think we were sexy."

"I was always surprised when people said I had a good groove, but I guess I did," says the classically inspired pianist/keyboardist Lisa Coleman, also a member of the Revolution.

"He called us his Mount Rushmore because we were iconic," says Revolution drummer Bobby Z. (born Robert B. Rivkin). "I think he knew that we could not have existed without each other."

If Prince was a puffy-blouse-wearing, make-up slathering, ring-tail rounder who toyed with an image of androgyny and mysterious sexuality, Revolution guitarist Wendy Melvoin and Lisa Coleman, known as Wendy and Lisa, were the real deal—two women in love who didn't toy with sexual identity, but lived life as a couple. That provoked Prince even more. "He played that up so well, embracing us and utilizing our sexuality to his advantage. It was the cherry—or two—on top of his sundae," says Coleman with a mischievous chuckle.

If Prince was a multi-tiered, multi-instrumentalist whose funk chops were as strong as his rock-outs, Revolution members Doctor Fink, Bobby Z., and bassist Brown Mark (born Mark Brown) were also there on the good foot, doubling down on whatever the boss meted out. "You had to be as good as him, if not better, because he wanted you to make him work," says Brown. "Plus, he was a real disciplinarian."

Whether the one man band of *For You*, Prince's debut album released in 1978 (its notes state he played all twenty-seven instruments), or its immediate follow-up, 1979's eponymous effort, may have led you to believe otherwise, Prince wrote, sang, and played best when playing to the strengths and quirks of that Revolution-ary team: guitarist Wendy Melvoin, bassist Brown Mark, drummer Bobby Z., keyboardist Matt "Doctor" Fink, and pianist/organist Lisa Coleman.

The Revolution was (and is) integral to Prince's 1979–1986 period, first with just Bobby Z. and Doctor Fink paired with André Cymone on bass, Dez Dickerson on guitar, and Gayle Chapman on keyboards and vocals. By 1980, Chapman was out and Coleman was in, playing keyboards on tour and singing "Head" on *Dirty Mind* with Prince. Melvoin joined the Revolution, first in 1982 for the album *1999* (the first time "the Revolution" appeared on an album cover of his) as a background singer at the insistence of Coleman. Melvoin jumped in on guitar when Dickerson left Prince's employ for religious reasons, and the Revolution blossomed in full, truly starting when this lineup made its live debut on August 3, 1983, at Minneapolis's First Avenue club, recording on and touring through *Purple Rain*, *Around the World in a Day*, *Parade*, and bits of *Sign "O" the Times* before Prince dissolved the Revolution in Japan on September 9, 1986. "That's classic Prince," notes Melvoin. "We're classic Prince."

Their funk matched his funk. Their acquaintance with the synthesizer-heavy new wave was as up close and personal as his. Their gauzy level of gender-fuck sexual playfulness matched his, guided by his hand, of course. They played their asses off, inventively, for him, while turning him on to new sounds, and Prince gave them a high point to live up to. "I don't really think he had ever fully listened to the Beatles until Matt and I played him *Sgt. Pepper's Lonely Heart Club Band*," says Bobby Z. "Wendy and Lisa presented him with jazz like he'd never heard. Classical and experimental music too; I mean, Lisa played sitar and flute as well as piano."

Listen to Prince pre–Wendy and Lisa. Then listen to him after, à la the *Revolver*-like *Around the World in a Day* and cabaret jazz elements of *Parade*. "He gave to us, and we gave to him in a free-flowing exchange of ideas," continues Z.

Sure, Prince was dashing and inventive without the Revolution. *The Black Album*, most of *Sign "O" the Times*, even a latter-day work such as the James Brown–ish *Musicology*: These aren't with the Revolution. "He sounded great on records without us, like *Diamonds and Pearls*," notes Fink.

"Some of the players after the Revolution could kick my ass," says Melvoin.

"But those don't really sound like him," notes Fink. "He doesn't sound like Prince. Who knows why?" Is Fink inferring that Prince doesn't sound like Prince because the Revolution wasn't there? "No, he just doesn't sound like my Prince."

The Revolution together with Prince: the sum of their funky, rocking, sensualist parts meant so much more as one grooving unit. There was charm, childlike wonder, and theatricalized naïveté. Prince had other bands after the Revolution, but never one that was a physical and psychic extension of everything that he was, such as this quintet. "I mean, he's had a lot of great players in his time, but none with the innocence and naïveté and growing pains we had with him," says Fink.

"We grew up together while working," says Coleman.

"We were young and came up as one," says Melvoin. "It's an intangible, really, oblique in its way, but we just worked together, lived together, were together."

This same older and wiser crew leapt quietly into the fire of tribute when Prince passed; first playing Prince's Minneapolis's original home base, the live venue First Avenue in September 2016, with a sold-out country-wide tour bringing them to the sad and hungry masses throughout 2017. "We're offering catharsis, not only for the audiences who loved him, but to ourselves, each other, because we were his family," says Melvoin. "We're emotional. We're hurting. We need a place to land."

Prince performs live onstage at Ritz-Carlton in New York on March 21, 1981, during the *Dirty Mind* tour. Drummer Bobby Z. and bassist André Cymone back him up. Photo by Richard E. Aaron/Redferns.

If you want emotion, try speaking to four grieving, yet excitable musicians baring their collective soul on one conference-call line over the course of several hours (Coleman would speak separately after this, with Melvoin and Fink offering additional information in secondary interviews).

The reunion tour is why "we're gathered for this thing called life," teases Bobby Z., quoting from Prince's "Let's Go Crazy," discussing how each managed to keep loose psychic contact with each other since Prince's dissolution of the whole. Each of them mentions how no one can or will replace Prince in their hearts, or in their upcoming stage show. "We hope the audience sings along," says Brown.

Each Revolution member recalls where they were and how they heard of Prince's death as if they were boomers reminiscing about the passing of John. F. Kennedy. "I was on the nineteenth song of my own album when I heard," says Brown. "I stopped immediately, put the thing on hold, and haven't looked back yet. This new adventure of the Revolution tour is too intriguing."

Fink was also working on music for a new streaming service in his office/studio when he saw a news report that someone had been found dead at Prince's Paisley Park complex. "I immediately thought of Prince—but didn't know for sure—figured 'no way,' then found out from a friend in the police department that it was him. My blood ran cold."

Wendy and Lisa are no longer romantically involved, yet remain a duo who score and record soundtracks for film and TV music (they won an Emmy in 2010 for their work on *Nurse Jackie*), and happened to be in the studio working on sounds for Jennifer Lopez's police drama, *Shades of Blue*, when word of Prince's demise reached them. "It really didn't seem possible, a dream perhaps, then—" Coleman trails off.

Drawn together for the first time in years (they've reunited several times without Prince since he parted ways with the Revolution, the last time being 2012), the three Minnesotans joined Coleman and Melvoin in a hotel room in Minneapolis to "hold each other" (a collective response) and grieve their friend and bandleader. "Things moved so quickly after he died that we weren't part of any formal ceremony," notes Melvoin who also claims that the Revolution weren't about to jump into the myriad tributes to Prince immediately following his passing. "The timing had to be right. It had to be unique and apart from everything else. We had to feel this," says Fink.

Feeling this, **uniquely and apart** from everything else, is how each player of the Revolution wound up playing at Prince's command. Technique was needed, but vibe was way more crucial to the then-baby-faced Prince. Everyone is short on dates and specifics but long and deep when it comes to emotional muscle memory.

Mark Brown laughs at how absolutely raw he was when he got to Prince, and how the guitarist—a notoriously demanding taskmaster who shifted tempos, literally, with a drop of a handkerchief—would command precision while insisting each player to be themselves and push him.

"When I came on board, André had already been with him for a minute and played bass a certain way," says Brown. "Prince never said why he hired me after all those other auditions, but I think it's because I was primal, that I had that Sly and the Family Stone rumble. He wanted someone who could play like him, but he also wanted someone who could take him higher, push him, help him to evolve."

Once Prince trusted that you had your sound and direction toward inventiveness and vibe down cold, he was set free to create, "to dress up whatever he wanted on guitar," stresses Brown. "That was his focus."

Bobby Z. was working as a studio drummer at producer Chris Moon's Moon Sound Studios in Minneapolis when Prince recorded his earliest tracks there in the late '70s. Moved by what he heard and witnessed from the young artist ("The first time I met him, he seemed truly mysterious, reptilian even"), Bobby Z. purposely went to work for Prince's first manager, Owen Husney, and quickly became Prince's "driver, gofer, and seeing-eye dog" during the daytime and jamming partner during the nights. "I wore him down, or he wore me down," Z. says and laughs. "He never slept." Two years of driving and schlepping paid off: Bobby became Prince's official drummer and the first real Revolution member.

Coleman's story of how she got to Prince—then eventually dragged her then-girlfriend Melvoin into the fold—is far funnier when told in full. "He already had a female in his band [Gayle Chapman] in 1979, but their personal relationship was falling apart, so she left." Like Dez, Chapman was religious and probably didn't dig simulating fellatio during "Head" while onstage. "Yet, he still wanted a woman in the band," says Coleman. "That was a big part of his vision. I'm still in high school, mind you—just graduating—and my best friend happened to get a job with his management in Los Angeles. She tells me about this opening in his band and for me to make a tape of myself, which I had never really done before."

It's important to note that both of Prince's non-Minneapolis Revolution members—Wendy and Lisa—were the immensely talented daughters of in-demand L.A. studio musicians and Wrecking Crew members: respectively, pianist Mike Melvoin who played and/or arranged for Frank Sinatra, John Lennon, and the Jackson 5; and percussionist Gary Coleman who played for Barbra Streisand and Marvin Gaye. "I've known Lisa since we were in diapers," says Melvoin. "I was, however, too young to join her first band with her brothers, Waldorf Salad."

There's also the fact that *Around the World in a Day* is littered with members of the Melvoin and Coleman fams, and that Wendy's twin sister, Susannah, was engaged to Prince in the mid-'80s, allegedly the focus of his "Nothing Compares 2 U." Of all the interpersonal connections, Brown laughs and says, "It's like going down a rabbit hole."

Back to Coleman: "I sent this tape to Prince of me singing and playing piano, and he received it on his birthday. Immediately, he sends for me to come to Minneapolis to play. He even picked me up at the airport. Remember, I'm pretty shy. Absolutely, I'm shy, so I probably looked down a lot. Apparently, that bothered Prince on the spot that I wouldn't look him in the eye. He thought this was so weird that when I got to his house and he pointed for me to go into the basement where the piano was, he jumped on the phone to his management to complain; something like, 'I don't know if it's going to work out with this weirdo.' Then, as he's on the phone, he heard me playing, and he told management, 'Forget that.' So, I dodged a bullet. I could have been sent home immediately all because I didn't look at him."

The eccentric Prince and the overly demanding Prince rarely come into play during these conversations. What did come to pass was the discussion of image—the questionable notions of sexual preference, the androgynous manner of glam Victoriana that was his costuming—when it came to being onstage, as well as being "the movie band," says Brown, referring to *Purple Rain*. "People really found us with that film," he says. "We became superstars just like Prince."

In many ways, what would become the visual image of the Revolution came naturally, and in league with who each player was. "I never saw someone who looked like a doctor, moved like a robot, and played like a demon," says Bobby Z. of Fink, who adds, "Doctor Fink is a character role that I came up with back in 1980. I was always happy with being the guy in scrubs, because Prince loved it and the scrubs are comfortable onstage. Even now, on tour, I will always be the Doctor."

The iconic *Purple Rain*–era Prince and the Revolution. Photo by Larry Williams, courtesy of Warner Bros.

Wendy Melvoin performing onstage with Prince and the Revolution at Ahoy, Rotterdam, Netherlands, August 17, 1986. Photo by Rob Verhorst/Redferns.

Lisa Coleman, photographed by Jeff Katz, from the cropped back cover of Prince's "Mountains" extended version 12-inch.

Photo courtesy of Warner Bros.

Brown likens what the Revolution was to Prince was like actors in a film, and not necessarily *Purple Rain*. To Prince, "I think [we] were like the cast of the original *Star Wars* with a Han Solo, a Princess Leia, [and] someone had to be a Chewbacca," he laughs. "He had us blocked and staged in his imagination."

With Melvoin and Coleman, things were trickier when it came to assigning roles that could involve skimpy, sheer lingerie. "Hmm, *assigned* probably isn't the right word," notes Melvoin. "He had a strong relationship to his own ideas of being a 'rock star.' He did, however, put the Revolution together and chose each one of us, not because we were a blank canvas. Each of us came to the table with self-possession and strong personalities. Sonically and visually, I believe Prince knew that we were all aspects of himself. Musically, though, that translated in a singular way when playing together. I might *never* have been comfortable with wearing lingerie, but I was comfortable being his female counterpart onstage. That was important to him."

Coleman wasn't exactly thrilled with the notion of teddies and garter belts ("I thought a bra, no shirt, and a jacket was sexy enough—funky, progressive, and risqué"), but did appreciate the outrageousness of it all. "That was a challenge though, to nudge each of us out of our comfort zone while highlighting who we were," she says. "He pushed and pushed to see how far he could go, how far we could go, and that put fire and energy into everything we did."

That Melvoin and Coleman were a gay couple, was—as Lisa noted previously—the cherry atop the icing of a very sexy sundae. With audiences already wondering if Prince was gay ("He loved that part of his mystique," notes Coleman), having lesbian musicians coupled up in the Revolution was something to take advantage of.

"We were so embracing and validating of his way in the world that [our relationship] created a beautiful atmosphere for him to be whoever and whatever he wanted to be," states Melvoin.

"It had to be a happy accident for him—like, 'Wow, this is my whole Black-White, male-female, gay-straight philosophy come to life,'" says Coleman. "That he had two women that were gay in his band was as if he had the jackpot."

Melvoin goes beyond the gay and color spectrum to include her own Jewishness into the mix of being part of a crazy, hungry group of misfits, not unlike Fleetwood Mac, Prince's ideal band model. According to Bobby Z., "When we first started at Warner [Bros.], they sent us all its product, and he really focused on that married-divorced, man-woman model. He got his Fleetwood Mac in us."

Fink goes on to say that, along with the music, Prince wished to pursue the notion of inclusivity and harmony. "For all his reliance on kink, he wanted to put that societal notion forward, that this rainbow nation was his playground."

Each Revolution member can easily focus on his or her favorite, most challenging musical moments: Melvoin selecting "When Doves Cry" for its complexity, Fink choosing "Purple Rain" for its epic emotionality, Z. mentioning "Darling Nikki" because its rhythmic interplay was nearly impossible to tackle onstage, and Brown fingering "Alexa De Paris," because it was "a *baaaaaaaad* song that proved all we could do."

What each member agreed upon, however—almost at once—was Coleman's sound and how it was so devastatingly original ("She was like a butterfly flitting," says Fink) that it frustrated Prince like no one else could. "Because he couldn't ever do what she did," laughs Melvoin. "He could do what rest of us did, kick our ass, and out-do us a hundred times over. Not Lisa. Lisa is a very tricky musician. She didn't study how to be Herbie Hancock, Arthur Rubenstein, or Sly Stone on the Hammond. She was just Lisa, studied only Lisa. And Prince could never approach or emulate or touch that. He had to admit that. He

coveted that. She was—and is—so good and so singular. He loved that."

Coleman appreciates the praise, calls herself "a classically trained hippie with an experimental jazz streak," and mentions how she could either move toward something avant-garde ("He counted on me to do the unexpected") or something deeply funky and righteously repetitious. "It was weird hearing that I was good with the groove, but that was necessary for us to be so around him. I remember one night at the end of "Controversy," jamming so hard and good, that we hit a height of perfection that made me cry—hysteria or joy that I felt as if I would explode, a whirling dervish high, a runner's high where everything floats effortlessly. We could play an eight-bar groove for hours while he worked out his guitar lines, playing with his microphone, or even his dance steps. We were like a machine. We became integral to every aspect of him."

This is where the problems may have come in for the Revolution, as with such dizzying heights—artistically and commercially after the mega-platinum success of *Purple Rain*—to maintain, Prince may have balked at going forward. "He definitely got bored of having to play *Purple Rain* all the time, which is why he released *Around the World in a Day* so soon during that tour," recalls Brown of the psych-pop effort, quick to share that ninety-eight percent of its tracks had already been recorded immediately following those of *Purple Rain*.

"You could tell he was in a hurry after going back-to-back with *Rain*, *World*, and *Parade*," says Z., who believes that Prince just wanted to move beyond whatever he was doing by any and all means necessary. "I think he was sick of his sound. Or bored."

"Lisa's harmonic conflicts started getting more twisted, clusters of notes start getting lovelier and not ugly sounding—she changed him," says Melvoin, hanging in mid-air. Were things getting too intense with Prince too reliant on the Revolution? "He never confided that in me," says Fink. "Prince didn't discuss much with me beyond music. However, I did try to dissuade him from going ahead with any wrong decisions like busting up the Revolution. Unbeknownst to me at that time, Mark Brown had already decided to leave the group in order to pursue a solo career and had signed to Motown Records."

Coleman believes that intensity of the Revolution may have just caught up to him unexpectedly, "because we had talked about doing so much more as a unit in the future." She understands artistic restlessness and Prince's relationship to stretching his boundaries. "We were so mutually involved in everything, on such even footing and moving forward, that there was no moving backwards—not for him, not for us. We were equals and were going to move forward in every way, *or* he could just fire us all and play with musicians he could control completely."

Without raising her voice, Coleman seems sad and angry at any notion of going backwards—not the lingerie or the show-business aspect of Prince's past endeavors. "He worried about that because he loved the show-biz aspect of it all, and we weren't trying to be outrageous anymore," says Coleman. "We were maturing, and my level of outrageousness was focused more on the musical, on that level of theatricality. What Prince wanted to do was get theatrical, but not so much musically, and certainly without us. And maybe I don't blame him. It was a show-biz decision. Look, the Revolution maintained purity and naïveté because Prince was all we knew. We started with Prince at a young age, and developed our egos and thick skins with him. We earned it—any other band that came after us, well, it was cake for them. Prince knew that in the Revolution he had a mirror that showed no other—that reflected him in every way. Maybe he just got tired of what he saw." ⊙

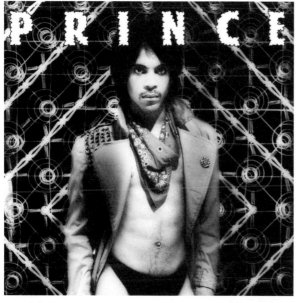

(*opposite*) Photo by Ed Thrasher. Courtesy of Warner Bros. (*above*) Albums recorded with a version of the Revolution band.

After the unprecedented success of *Purple Rain*, Prince quickly followed it up with
AROUND THE WORLD IN A DAY, his quirkiest release so far.

FLY BY NIGHT

by A. D. Amorosi

Prince should have been over the moon with *Purple Rain*, his sixth studio album and the first to feature the Revolution. Released on June 25, 1984, with a tour (the first to feature Melvoin as the new guitarist) split into two legs and lasting into 1985, Prince could have kept the platinum-plated momentum going for the rousing *Rain*. "Except that he was restless and bored by halfway through the tour," says Fink.

What Prince did to alleviate such boredom was return to a piece of music that came his way before the utopian, new-wave gospel of *Purple Rain*: a demo of "Around the World in a Day" provided to him by Lisa Coleman's brother David, who would eventually play oud, cello, and more on what would become the title track of Prince's new album. David would play on "Raspberry Beret" and "The Ladder" as well, and Melvoin's brother Jonathan and twin sister, Susannah, also played and sang during the *Around the World in a Day* sessions.

"These songs were such a left turn creatively and lyrically from anything that came before it that, at first, it was hard to tackle," says Fink. "Technically, everything here was on another level. For instance, 'Condition of the Heart,' was all just *feel*. No definite tempo with that intro. Very abstract. Doing that live was bizarre." Fink states that much of this album sounded random and difficult to emulate onstage: "Maybe the hardest of all his albums, really. Some of it sounded like a butterfly flitting through the breeze." Melvoin goes on to say that "any of Prince's music with finesse and dynamic, such as *Around the World*, was rougher to play."

Influenced by Coleman and Melvoin's classicism, jazz chops, and experimental nature, Prince—never a pronounced Beatles fan—dove into Liverpudlian psychedelia with relish. But not before he initially resisted the outside inspiration, according to Melvoin. "It was eons before we recorded it that my brother gave me the tape of that song," she says. "Lisa and I dragged Prince outside the studio and made him listen to this cassette in a car… I don't even remember whose car, but man, that was a scene. As soon as Prince heard it though, he loved it; so much so that when he had the chance, he changed his whole direction toward *that*."

Prince hadbecome increasingly reliant upon Wendy and Lisa as musicians and friends, a fact that may have bothered Fink, who had known and played with the guitarist since 1980. "No, I liked those two and had other sessions at the time that I was involved in," says Fink. "It is true that if Prince called—even if it was 3:00 AM—and you weren't ready, he was pissed. He had no call to be angry at me, and worked with me all the time. That was the most important thing. Besides, Prince and I didn't have a conversational relationship. Like, I remember being on tour during the Reagan era, and asking him what he thought about things. He acted as if we shouldn't discuss politics or religion."

Instead, Prince funneled his opinionated take on politics, nuclear weaponry, money, and anti-Communist rhetoric on songs such as "America" and his cryptic views on all-that-was Heaven on the spacey ballad "The Ladder" and the grouchy, noise-R&B of "Temptation."

Then there was "Pop Life," the bubbling poppy funk-lite look into Prince's ever-widening disgust with fame, a swipe at stardom that surprised Fink to his core. "We did work so long to get there," he says. "He's a cynical guy, but this seemed more crusty than usual. Then again, I'm not sure he liked his privacy invaded or having to think about success as opposed to just music, pure and simple."

One of the most unique elements of the *Around the World* project was Prince's welcoming of his father, pianist John L. Nelson, into the fold. In the film *Purple Rain*, the character based upon Nelson is distant and cold, yet it is his death by suicide that prompts Prince to write the title track and dedicate it to his late father. "I'm not completely sure what bad had ever transpired between Prince and his dad, but he used to hang out with us all the time and was nothing but lovely," says Fink. "He was extremely gracious toward the band, and to me, in particular. Also [he] had helpful commentary and was supportive. I liked that. Not a negative bone or critical toward Prince in any way. When we did 'The Ladder,' I felt as Mr. Nelson was there to influence his son, make everything better."

Ask Fink what he thinks of *Around the World in a Day*, and the keyboardist believes that it shows Prince's lightest touch as a composer and arranger, despite the cynicism and cryptic lyrics. "Look, he could have kept making *Purple Rain*s. We had, like, forty additional songs from that album alone. He *wanted* to do *Around the World* to clear the air, change the dial. I think he thought, 'Oh my God, *Purple Rain* is my *Thriller*. Now what? I'll never top it, so I'll just experiment, change direction, and reinvent the wheel.' And he never stopped doing that for the rest of his career." ●

(*opposite*) Original promo sticker for *Around the World in a Day*.

51

While *Purple Rain* is considered Prince and the Revolution's peak, Prince never went backwards, only up, and PARADE climbed mighty heights as the Revolution's final album together. Engineer Susan Rogers, bouncing between two studios and a mobile unit, witnessed the entire ascent. Producer/engineer David Z mixed the music for the accompanying film, *Under the Cherry Moon*, and lent a hand in creating the smash hit "Kiss."

THE MOUNTAIN

by Chris Williams

When and where did you first meet Prince?

David Z: I met Prince in Minneapolis when he was fifteen. To make a long story short, I did the demo that got him signed to Warner Bros. Records. First, he recorded with Chris Moon, then he got a new manager named Owen Husney, and he brought him to me. We did the four songs that got him signed. Those songs ended up on his first record: "Soft and Wet," "Baby," and a couple other songs. This is when I first met him. He was very young back then. We didn't know if he was going to become a star or anything. We did it because the music sounded good. His first album didn't really sell, and his second album did a little better, then he started to hit his groove, and that is when things started to pick up. I met him before he was signed to the record label. I was twenty-nine or thirty when I met him.

Susan Rogers: At the time, I was in Los Angeles working for Crosby, Stills & Nash. I was their studio technician. I had been a Prince fan, and a fan of R&B and soul music since I was a little kid. So I was aware of Prince. He was my favorite artist, and I followed his career. I saw him a couple times in concert. I saw his *Controversy* and *Dirty Mind* tours. I was just a big fan. I heard through the professional grapevine via other technicians in Hollywood that Prince was looking for an audio technician. And that's what I was at the time. This was in the summer of 1983. As soon as I heard about the opportunity, I applied for the job. Westlake Audio was assigned the task of finding Prince a technician. So I went to Glenn Phoenix, the head of Westlake Audio, and he knew me because my boyfriend worked for him at the time. I said to him, "Glenn, I want that job! I want that job!" He interviewed me, and he told me, "Yeah. You're perfect. You'll do." Then they sent me over to Prince's management, and Steve Fargnoli interviewed me

and he said, "All right. I think Prince will like you, because he likes working with women." I was fully qualified for the job as well. We discussed what my salary would be and they said okay, and off I went. I was hired before I ever met him. I went out to Minneapolis and began working for him. I first met him on the job.

Westlake Audio sent me and some other people out to Prince's house, and this was his old house on Kiowa Trail in Chanhassen, Minnesota. Ultimately, he painted it purple, and eventually he gave it to his father, John Nelson. This was the summer of 1983. Prince just wrapped up his *1999* tour. He was planning the *Purple Rain* movie and album. They sent me out to his house with some new equipment. We delivered a new API recording console and a few other odds and ends. The first time I ever laid eyes on him in person, he was actually in a towel and wearing a shower cap. [*laughs*] It was by accident. I was out in the driveway. We were unloading equipment off the truck, and I needed to use the restroom. Prince's secretary named Sandy Scipioni said to me, "Oh. Just go in the house. Go in the front door." I walked through the front door, and this little figure came flying past me around the corner and down the stairs to the master bedroom. It was Prince. He was wearing a towel and a shower cap, because he just got out of the shower. [*laughs*] I was saying to myself that this is not good, because I didn't want him to think I was trying to embarrass him. He didn't even see me.

When I first went to work with him, I spent my first week installing a new console and repairing a tape machine in the basement of his home. So, if you can imagine a split-level house, the master bedroom was down a half flight of stairs. It was somewhat underground because the house was on a hill. If you entered the front door from the street level, it was a one-level, but his bedroom was about a half-floor down. Across the hallway from his master bedroom was another bedroom,

(*opposite*) Photograph by Jeff Katz. Courtesy of Warner Bros.

53

which became his recording studio, where, surprisingly, he did a lot of the tracks for the *1999* and *Purple Rain* albums. So I was in that bedroom studio taking out an old console and rewiring a new console and repairing the tape machine for about a week. I could hear him upstairs. Directly above me were the kitchen, dining room, and living room, and his piano was on that floor. I could hear him working on parts for "Computer Blue" and "The Beautiful Ones." He was working out parts on the piano right above me. He was waiting for me to finish the installation so he could begin recording. I finally finished it, and I still hadn't met him face-to-face yet. The only person I'd dealt with was Sandy Scipioni.

So I called Sandy, and I said, "Sandy, I'm finished. Let him know that he can use the studio now." She called him, and he came downstairs to see me. It was kind of late in the evening. It was after a long workday. He gave me some instructions, and I told him the room was ready to go. This was the first time I talked to him, and as he was about to walk back upstairs, a little voice inside of me said, "Don't let it start like this." As he was going back upstairs, I said, "Prince." He stopped and turned around. I stuck my hand out for a handshake. I said, "My name is Susan Rogers." It was just instinctive for me to do that. I just moved 2,300 miles away from home and left everything to come there. I didn't want this guy to start telling me what to do without me telling him my name. We shook hands, and he thought it was kind of funny. He was trying not to laugh, and he said, "I'm Prince." [*laughs*] I think he kind of liked that, but that's how I met him and started working for him, but things got off to a slow start though.

I remember shortly after that he had Jesse Johnson and Morris Day come over to the house to start working on some of the Time's stuff. The three of them were talking about music, and I was being quiet, very respectful, and doing what I was told and trying to fit in. I was a White girl from Southern California, but they didn't know that I knew all their references. I knew every obscure record they were talking about. I listened to the same music. At one point, Morris mentioned Frankie Beverly and Maze and One Way featuring Al Hudson. They mentioned a particular song that I knew, and I was like, "Oh!" because I loved that song. I remember all three of them looked up, and I looked at them, and it was a form of silent communication. It was like, "Yeah. I know what you know." We had the same frame of reference. After that, things changed. I felt like I hadn't gained full entrance into the club, but I, at least, came closer to the inner circle. Not all his employees listened to the same music they did. I knew many of the same cultural references and that helped me a great deal in that position.

By knowing the same cultural and musical references, how did that experience assist you in the recording process and capturing the overall sound for Prince?

Susan Rogers: I think Prince was grateful that, not only did he have a woman engineer, but a woman that knew what he had listened to growing up and had a similar value system. I joined him as an audio technician, but he knew that he could mold me into becoming the engineer he wanted because we liked the same things. At the very least, it helped that I knew the music of James Brown, Sly and the Family Stone, and Parliament-Funkadelic. I knew what he was going for. I think he felt a little bit more comfortable with me, knowing that I enjoyed the music that we were making, and that I wasn't just sitting there secretly wishing we were making acoustic folk or rock music. What we were making was what I wanted to hear.

Going into the making of *Parade*, Prince was coming off a stellar year in 1984 with *Purple Rain*, and another successful album in 1985 with *Around the World in a Day*. This album became the last one he released with the Revolution. Can you describe his new focus, direction, and sound with this album?

David Z: Well, the *Parade* record was the soundtrack for his second movie, *Under the Cherry Moon*. Honestly, I didn't have a lot to do with many songs on the album, although I mixed them for the movie. The only real song I did anything on was [the smash hit] "Kiss." On all the other songs, Prince was doing everything himself. We were at Sunset Sound Studio in Los Angeles. He was working in Studio 3 like he usually did, and I was working in Studio 2. I was producing a group for him called Mazarati. He was giving us songs every once in a while. We did a few of his songs that were meant for the Time. He wasn't with them anymore. He gave me a demo of him playing an acoustic guitar with just the first verse and chorus of "Kiss." We didn't know what to do with it because it sounded like a funk song. We programmed the drums, and I did the guitar part, which I [triggered the sample of it on] a hi-hat on the drum set. It's kind of technical. I put it through a delay unit and altered the delay from the original signal to the delayed signal to halfway. It created a rhythm which was really funky. No one could really play that rhythm because it was very difficult, but then I played the acoustic guitar and gated it to that, so it made that funky rhythm that everyone hears today.

We did the song for Mazarati, and they sang it an octave lower. We had a lot of stuff on there. There was some bass and a full piano part. After we did the song, I went back to the hotel and came back the next morning and the tape was gone. I asked my assistant, "Where is the tape?" [*laughs*] He replied, "Prince took it." I went into his studio and he had already sung the song and played that James Brown lead guitar on it. "Papa's Got a Brand New Bag" had the same beginning, but he said, "It was too good for you guys, so I took it back." [*laughs*] What was I going to say? I was promised a co-producer credit on the album, but you know how that goes. But I created this rhythm track that he made into his own song. It was great. No one else could've sung it like he did. This is how this song came together. I think it was an afterthought, because the album was already done. He added "Kiss" at the last minute because he liked it so much. We already listened to the rest of the album, so I knew it was done and mixed, but that's what happened with this song. This was really the only thing I had to do with the *Parade* record, except when *Under the Cherry Moon* was made, I mixed the whole record for the film.

Susan Rogers: There was the artistic pressure to change and grow. He hit a homerun with *Dirty Mind* because it was the right aesthetic. He hit a home run with *1999*, and he really nailed it with *Purple Rain*. The pressure on an artist to do that again is very great, because you have to make the right work of art at the right time. He liked the whole black-and-white aesthetic at the time we were recording this album. He was trying to do a new movie, and he was thinking more globally. He was thinking about the South of France and Europe. He was thinking about increasing his profile, but it was such a gamble. He was such a smart and intuitive guy. He got it nearly perfect with his *Parade* record. The movie *Under the Cherry Moon* wasn't a hit, but the album was a very, very strong album. What people were hearing was an attempt by a man who was very successful but wasn't willing to cloak himself in the mantle of success and just rest on his laurels. He was still trying to come up with something new artistically. He was trying to get new sounds and looking for new lyrical statements. He was still reaching for something.

Producer David Z (aka David Rivkin) in the studio in Minneapolis, Minnesota, April 1989. Photo by Jim Steinfeldt/Michael Ochs Archives/Getty Images.

I was producing a group for Prince called Mazarati. He gave me a demo of "Kiss." We programmed the drums, and I did the guitar part. After we did the song, I came back the next morning and the tape was gone. Prince said, "It was too good for you guys, so I took it back."

It was a more collaborative atmosphere on *Around the World in a Day* than *Parade*. Most of the songs on *Parade* were done by Prince alone. The song "Mountains" is a shining example. The genesis of "Mountains" was done by Wendy and Lisa. The three of us did the basic track in London on our own. Prince sent Wendy and Lisa to London, and he rented a flat and bought them some studio time, and he sent me with them, so we could do some recording. We did the tracks for "Mountains" and "Power Fantastic." We brought them back to Prince, and he added the lyrics and finished up the tracks. So there weren't really collaborations on the *Parade* record. It was more of a solo endeavor. He had Wendy and Lisa collaborate quite a bit in terms of playing instruments and singing, but he was telling them what to play, with the exception of "Sometimes It Snows in April." That song was a true collaboration. For "Sometimes It Snows in April," he put Lisa on piano and Wendy on guitar. He gave them the chord changes and the direction, and he let them do what they did best. But the other songs on the record pretty much reflect Prince alone, other than "Mountains." *Sign "O" the Times* was a little more collaborative with Sheila E., and *Around the World in a Day* was more collaborative with the band; but *Parade* was pretty much a solo expression for Prince, now that I think about it.

What about the two songs his father received credit for on this album?

Susan Rogers: His father's inclusion wasn't really an artistic inclusion. The truth of the matter was that he wanted his father to get a little bit of money. Prince's father inspired him in many, many ways, so Prince would give his father songwriting credits on songs, in order for his father to get some royalty checks. His father may have played something on the piano that Prince then turned into a song. I'm not saying his dad wasn't an artist or a piano player or an inspiration in his own right, but those songwriting credits were sometimes a little bit of a stretch. I recorded John Nelson a couple times, and he was a jazz piano player, but he tended to ideate and riff and move from one theme to another. He didn't have a lot of cohesive ideas in his music, but that's not to say that Prince didn't take some of those ideas and some of his chord progressions and turn them into melodies. I think John Nelson is where Prince got a lot of his genius for melodies.

Can you describe the studio atmosphere that existed during the making of this album?

David Z: Prince had two rooms booked at Sunset Sound. It was kind of like a beehive. There was activity everywhere. There was a basketball court outside. When everyone took a break, we'd go outside and shoot baskets. We'd go in one studio or another. I don't think Mazarati went into Prince's studio very much, but he'd come over to see how his project was going. It was a very creative beehive back then. I think that is what he was trying to create with Paisley Park when he built it. Everyone was interacting, which was really great because it inspired our creativity. There were other people in other rooms making music. That is really important for creativity. I think sitting at home alone making a beat is a little stifling. Music is supposed to be made with other people. There was friendly competition back then.

Susan Rogers: It was pretty quiet. He didn't narrate his process. He would come into the studio with an idea for a melody or lyric, but he wouldn't say it. He'd like to have all his instruments set up and ready to go before he arrived to the studio. He would either give me instructions by phone or leave a written note in the studio saying,

"Here is what I want set up." He would describe whether or not it was going to be live or acoustic drums or a drum machine, or what kind of guitar sound he wanted: distorted or clean, or which keyboard he wanted set up. What that meant was, when he walked into the studio, he wanted to be able to go from the drums to bass to keys to guitars and move through each instrument expressing his ideas. As I recall, he did most of his experimenting midway through the songs. So, he would come in with a pretty good idea of what the basic rhythm track should be, then he'd spent a good bit of the time in the middle, experimenting with different guitar and keyboard sounds. After that, there would be a pause where he would stop and go out to his car with the tape to write lyrics, or he would already have the lyrics, and we would keep on going, and he would sing the song and do all the background parts. Then we would spend the rest of the time mixing and adding the final instrumentation.

Sometimes, he would call Eric Leeds to play the saxophone or Wendy, Lisa, or other people to come in to do backing vocals. For the most part, he was doing nearly everything himself. He would move through it as if he had the song pretty much fleshed out in his head, as we were going along. No one had any way of knowing how much of that was true. I could tell when he was experimenting, because he'd try one song, then he'd skip it and go to another. But it's pretty safe to say that he had a very high capacity to imagine songs and be able to craft them. Any time an artist creates a work of art, there is art involved, which serves as inspiration, but the rest of it is going to be craft. Ninety percent of it will be craft. It's impossible to say, when he came into the studio, how much of it was art, like how much of his inspiration started in his alone time versus how much of the art came to him, as he was in the process of making the record. I have a little bit of a hunch, but no one will ever know for sure. Some tracks we did just to dance to. Those are ones where he clearly didn't have any songs in mind. He was just laying down a groove. Then he'd come up with some stupid lyrics, and those were tracks that didn't end up on the album. For other tracks that were more important, I got the sense that he would come in with a strong idea. In another words, he would've done the creative part on his own—the actual thinking part. What I would do with him during that time period was the craft of actually making it come into reality.

Did Prince have a set time where he would come into the studio to work?

Susan Rogers: Any time he could, which meant if he was awake and not in a business meeting or on a date, he was in the studio. If we were on tour at the end of a set in an arena, he would come off the stage and take a shower at the hotel and change clothes. Then, sometimes he'd play an after-party, or if he didn't, we would go into the studio to start recording. Every chance he had, he would be in the studio. When we were doing the *Under the Cherry Moon* movie, there was a mobile truck on the movie set, so when the French crew were taking their two-hour lunches, he could be in the mobile truck recording. Studio sessions were frequently twenty-four hours long. Twenty hours was a fairly typical day. Twelve hours would feel like a day off. [*laughs*] But we would just keep on going and going until the song was done. Sometimes, we would go to bed at six o'clock in the evening or at six o'clock in the morning. We'd sleep for a few hours, then take care of some business and go back into the studio. We really lost track of time. We didn't know if it was day or night, but it didn't *matter*. It was a cycle of sleeping, eating, and recording in the studio. That's what we did all the time.

PRINCE AND THE R

EVOLUTION / PARADE

Artist: Prince and the Revolution
Album: *Parade*
Label: Paisley Park
Release year: 1986
Performed, arranged, produced, and composed by: Prince and the Revolution
Orchestra composed and arranged by: Clare Fischer
Engineered by: David Z, Susan Rogers, Coke Johnson, David Leonard, David Tickle, and Peggy Mac
Recorded at: Paisley Park and Sunset Sound (Los Angeles)
Orchestra recorded at: Monterey Sound by Arne Frager
Cover photo by: Jeff Katz

Where does the Revolution enter into the creative framework for this album?

Susan Rogers: The band was never in the studio before Prince. Everything would start with him. It also depended where we were. About fifty-five percent of the time, we were in Minneapolis, because that's where he liked to be, it's where he lived, and we had a rehearsal space. I had recording consoles hooked up to the rehearsal space. So that meant the whole band could be there rehearsing, and I could be recording what the band was playing. It wasn't the typical recording studio, but it allowed Prince to record ideas, as they came to him, with the whole band in rehearsal. We would lay down tracks that way. In those cases, a record would start with the whole band playing, then he would send the band home. He and I would do the vocals and overdubs. Sometimes, he'd have Wendy and Lisa stay around or Eric Leeds to finish certain parts that he needed done, but he liked to work by himself. Most of the time, in Los Angeles at Sunset Sound and many tracks at home, [the process] would start with just him. The only time he would bring in Wendy and Lisa was when he needed their special touch. Lisa played piano in a way that he didn't. Wendy played guitar in a way that he didn't. Often, he would bring them in for backing vocals. Most times, it was just he and I. He would play everything, so they weren't always involved in the records.

How much of the recording took place in Europe?

Susan Rogers: We did a little bit of work in a couple studios in the South of France. We had this mobile truck where we did a few pieces here and there, but all the pieces we worked on didn't end up on the album. We did songs like "Splash," "Sexual Suicide," "Power Fantastic," and a few things there. He didn't get a chance to devote his energies to the *Parade* album until he finished the movie. He did a lot of ideation, and he got a lot of inspiration when he was in Europe, but he didn't really start recording until we returned home when he could get into Sunset Sound in Los Angeles and at his home studio in Minneapolis. That's where he liked to work and where his ideas really flowed. We worked at Advision Studios in London for a day or two,

then we worked in that Advision truck in the South of France. But the real work was done at Sunset Sound and at home in Minneapolis.

What were some of the similarities and differences between recording at Sunset Sound and at his home studio in Minneapolis?

Susan Rogers: As far as the signal path went, it was pretty good at home. We had really good equipment at his home studio in Minneapolis, but Sunset Sound is one of the great studios of the world. When we worked there, we had everything. We had every tube microphone, the greatest equipment, and a maintenance staff. We had everything that money could buy. Sunset Sound was the pinnacle. It is legendary. When we worked at home, we had good equipment, but we didn't have the same support we could get at Sunset. When Prince worked in Minneapolis, he had a different kind of freedom. The vibe was different between the two studios. As far as the auditory path, it was the same at both places.

What was some of the equipment you used during your recording sessions?

Susan Rogers: At Sunset Sound and Prince's home studio, we had custom recording consoles made by a guy named Frank DeMedio. Frank designed this console for Studio 3 at Sunset Sound. It was basically an API design, but it was customized by Frank. Prince liked it so much that he had Frank build one for his home. So we used that API DeMedio recording console at Sunset and at home. At Sunset Sound, we used Studer tape machines. At home in Minneapolis, we used an MCI tape machine because it was reliable and I could fix it. I was out there by myself, and there were no other technicians around. We had the nice outboard gear he liked. We had an EMT reverb unit and a Telefunken U47 tube microphone in both places. He liked those mics a lot. We had all the usual stuff other studios had. We had harmonizers. He loved the Lexicon Prime Time [Delay] and Lexicon 480L Reverb. The equipment itself wasn't unusual, but the way he used it was definitely unique.

PRINCE AND THE REVOLUTION/KISS

SIDE ONE
KISS
(Prince)
SIDE TWO
♥ OR $
(Prince And The Revolution)
"KISS" PRODUCED, COMPOSED AND PERFORMED
BY PRINCE AND THE REVOLUTION
"Kiss" arranged by David Z.
Background Voice by Mazarati
"♥ OR $" PRODUCED, ARRANGED, COMPOSED AND PERFORMED
BY PRINCE AND THE REVOLUTION

Original version
of "Kiss" available on
the forthcoming album PARADE,
MUSIC FROM THE WARNER BROS. MOTION
PICTURE UNDER THE CHERRY MOON,
available on LP (1-25395),
cassette (4-25395)
and Compact Disc (2-25395).
45 RPM

Take me through the studio setup. Where did Prince typically record, and where were you situated during the recording process?

Susan Rogers: He liked to move quickly in the studio. Typically, the drums would be in another room in the studio. The control room is where the console was located. The drums had to be on the other side of the glass. Because Prince played every instrument, he liked to have his guitar running direct in the control room. He liked to have as many keyboards as possible in the control room. He wanted to have the piano miked up all the time, so that any point he could jump out and play acoustic piano, as opposed to electronic keyboard. He liked to have his microphone in the control room, because he wanted to do his vocals by himself. After we would lay down the bed track of drums, bass, and the basic rhythm instruments, the next thing he wanted to do was his vocal. So he would do his vocal when the song was about halfway done. To do his vocal, I would set up his vocal path; meaning, in the control room, I would set up the microphone he liked on a boom stand, and then I'd route it through whatever preamp and compressor or limiter. And both of us liked using the Urei LA-2A, and he'd be all set up and ready to go so he could record his vocals alone in the control room. All he had to do was switch tracks if he wanted to punch himself in and out of record. So the engineer [and] I, or whoever was working with him, would leave the control room, and he would do his lead vocal alone. Then we would come back in, and he'd do his backing vocals and the remainder of the overdubs, sitting in the control room behind the console. Often while he was playing keyboards or guitar, I would be playing the console, shaping sounds, EQing, compressing, adding reverb, and adding delay, dialing in the sound. By the time we finished the final overdubs, the song would be nearly ready to go. Then we would mix it, and we'd print it, and it'd be done.

This was different from how most artists worked. In a typical day, most artists could spend twelve hours at the studio. In a twelve-hour day, most artists could do two or three parts, because it took artists so long to come up with ideas; but if an artist is able to get a couple guitar parts done in a day in a studio, that was a good day for every record maker during the golden era of record making. But Prince, in the same amount of time, could do half a song in twelve hours. In twenty-four hours, the song would be done. It would be mixed and everything. We worked exceptionally fast, sometimes to our detriment. Prince wasn't a perfectionist, contrary to popular belief. He was not a perfectionist. He would've never been able to put out that much *stuff* if he had been a perfectionist. He was prolific. He wrote *a lot*. Pound for pound, that guy had more ideas than any popular music maker *ever*. So what Prince needed was not perfection, because that would've slowed him down. What he needed was facilitation. He needed someone to facilitate the working process so he could get his ideas out really fast, which is why in the '80s I was a very useful person to him, because I wasn't going to get hung up on the details of engineering. I was just going to help him to get it done. Prince was one-of-a-kind. There was no one like him. He was a true genius.

Let's delve into some of the singles released from this album.

David Z: For "Kiss," there was only nine tracks used for that song. There was twenty-four tracks, but we only used nine. The drum pattern was out of a machine called the Linn LM-1 drum machine. We had a kick drum on one track and everything else on the other tracks: snare, tongs, and hi-hats. There was one bass track. The instrument I used was: I gated the hi-hat through a delay unit to make

a rhythm. I put the acoustic guitar through the gate and triggered it with the hi-hat. So what it does is, it slows down the track, only when the hi-hat is hitting, then it shuts down the guitar track. And it shuts it off, when it's not appearing. That resulted in the rhythm that became infectious on the track. The piano part I stole from a Bo Diddley song called "Say Man." The background vocals I stole from Brenda Lee's song called "Sweet Nothin's." Prince put a lead guitar on there, which was beautiful, and he sang it. Then, while we were mixing it, he said we didn't need the bass or piano part, so it became this bare-bones thing. I reached over and snuck the piano in some places. In the end, I don't think we used all nine tracks for the song. We didn't put any echo or reverb on the song. There was some reverb on the kick sound that actually filled up the bass spot, so we didn't need the bass anymore. The song was very different from anything else he had done to that point in his career. When he gave the song to Warner Bros. to make it the single, I received a call from the A&R there and he said, "Prince really fucked up." I replied, "What?" He said, "Yeah. Prince fucked up. We're not going to release that. It sounds like a demo. There is no bass, no echo. There's nothing. It sucks." I hung up the phone, and I was so brokenhearted. I was really down. Luckily enough, Prince had enough pull because of *Purple Rain*. He told Warner Bros., "You're going to put that out, or I'm not giving you another single." So they had to put it out, reluctantly. A year later, all they were trying to do was to find songs just like "Kiss." It was cool for me to be involved musically with the creation of Prince's song.

Susan Rogers: On "Kiss," we were at Sunset Sound, and [Revolution bassist] Brown Mark had a band that were friends of his that he was bringing up through the ranks. They were called Mazarati. They were a local Minneapolis band. I think Prince signed them to Paisley Park Records. While Prince and I were working in Studio 3 at Sunset Sound, Prince booked time for Brown Mark and David Z in Studio 2 across the courtyard to work with Mazarati on their album. They needed another song for it. So Prince and I stopped what we were doing, and Prince took an acoustic guitar, which was something he almost never did, but he picked up this Ovation acoustic guitar and he banged out this song really fast. We put it on cassette. It was really a demo recording, which is also something else he never did. It was him doing the basic idea for "Kiss" on acoustic guitar. We sent the tape over to Studio 2. David Z and Brown Mark came up with this great track, and the guys from Mazarati did the backing vocals. David Z came up with the famous chords for the song. They brought the track back, and Prince freaked out. He loved it so much. He was laughing when he said, "I'm taking that back! I'm taking that back!" [*laughs*] We took the tape back. It sounded great. They did a great job. Prince put his lead vocal on it, and we did the overdubs. Kudos go to Brown Mark and David Z. It was Prince's song, but it was another collaboration for sure.

On "Anotherloverholenyohead," I loved this song so much! It was one of the many songs that he banged out so fast. The unusual guitar sound on it came from this weird instrument made by Roland. Roland tried to make a MIDI guitar. It was horrible. Prince had an early one. It was really crap, because it wouldn't track well. He would play a certain thing, but the sound that came out wouldn't track your hand movements. It was really unpredictable. It was impossibly difficult to play. But he was able to coax enough sound out of it that we were able to get the lead line for that song. He came up with that beautiful piano part at the end of it. It was a really nice track.

"Girls & Boys" came together very quickly. It was a very strong song, and it was obvious that it was going to be one of the singles released from the album. It also featured the same Roland MIDI guitar thing as well.

(*above*) Eric Leeds and Prince during the *Parade* tour at Wembley Arena, London, August 1986. Photo by Michael Putland/Getty Images.
(*opposite*) Wendy Melvoin and Miko Weaver during the *Parade* tour at Vorst Nationaal, in Brussels, Belgium, August 27, 1986.
Photo by Gie Knaeps/Getty Images.

Can you take me through your process of mixing the songs from this album for the 1986 movie *Under the Cherry Moon*?

David Z: To mix songs for a film is different than mixing them for an album. To mix for a record, you mix left, right, and stereo. For film, you mix left, center, right, and then surround. Back then, we were using something called a Dolby box, which routed some of the sound to the surround speakers in the back of the movie theater. Anything you pan left to right is going to be shadowed in the surround speakers a little bit. It's kind of a different kind of mix because we had to have eight channels. We premixed down to an eight-track machine. We had drums left and right. The guitar parts were on two tracks. The keyboard parts were divided on two tracks. The background vocals were divided on two tracks. The lead vocal was on one track and the effects were on two separate tracks; so when we went in to mix the movie, there was only eight tracks that were like submasters. Then you can mix it in a theater setting. We mixed it at Todd-AO Studio back then. It was a movie theater that didn't have any seats in it. We mixed music on one board, dialogue on another board, and sound effects on the other board. There were three sets of people working to combine all the elements. It was pretty fun.

During the mixing of the movie, I walked up to the mix studio one day, and I had to walk through the movie lot. At that time, I saw Prince talking to somebody. The person's back was towards me. As I got closer, I was holding these big, heavy reels of tape, and as I walked up, I saw it was Michael Jackson. [*laughs*] I was in awe. Prince said, "David, do you know Michael?" I replied, "No. I don't." Michael said, "Hi, how are you?" I shook his hand. But I was still carrying these heavy tapes, and I didn't want to interrupt their conversation. I said to Michael, "It was nice to meet you." As I turned to leave, I heard Prince say, "Michael, he's too busy to talk to you." [*laughs*] That was his sense of humor. He said it so I could hear it. It was funny. I don't know what they were talking about. After they were done talking, they both walked into the movie mix studio with their bodyguards. Prince had that guy named Chick, and he was huge. Michael had his bodyguard too. The mix and movie were looking and sounding good. Prince was happy.

There was a Ping-Pong table set up in the middle of the big screen and the board. This was a huge, movie-sized theater room. Prince was very competitive, and he loved Ping-Pong. He asked Michael, "Do you want to play Ping-Pong?" Michael replied, "I don't know how to play, but I'll play." So they started playing Ping-Pong in front of us while we were working. I was in the process of mixing, and it was really distracting. It wasn't just two regular people playing Ping-Pong. Everybody looked at each other, and we were like, "That's Prince and Michael Jackson playing Ping-Pong!" At one point, Prince asked Michael, "Do you want me to slam it?" Michael replied, "Yeah. Okay." Prince slams the ball and Michael drops the paddle and puts his hands in front of his face to protect his face. The game was over then. Michael walked out with his bodyguard and Prince was strutting around saying, "Did you see that? He played like Helen Keller." He was so proud. [*laughs*] It was just the way he was. He was a very funny guy. He had a great sense of humor. We used to do all kinds of practical jokes, which if he was still alive, he wouldn't want me to tell.

What was one of the practical jokes that you guys pulled off together?

David Z: We'd go out to these fancy restaurants with these white tablecloths. We'd bring a mini squirt gun, and we'd take turns lifting up the tablecloth and squirting up in the air over the tables next to

us while laughing. Some guy would be wiping his head and saying "What the hell?" After a couple times, one of the guys called the waiter over and said, "You know, your air-conditioning is broken. It is leaking all over me." [*laughs*] We laughed our asses off. It was typical of the fun we had together. It was so hard because we couldn't burst out loud laughing. They would've known something was up, if we did. We couldn't stop smiling during the whole dinner. It was great.

Do you have another one of those stories?

David Z: I have a few. I'll give you a short one. One day, he called me out to his house. He had a studio in his house on the lake in Minnesota. I drove out to his house, and for some reason, it was ninety-eight degrees that day. I wore a really loud Hawaiian shirt with palm trees, toucan birds, island greens and blues. I never wore stuff like that. I came into the studio and he said, "We're going to edit 'Erotic City.'" That was the name of the song he was working on. We had to cut it down because it was really long. So the tape machine I was cutting on was underneath these big, huge speakers that were in the ceiling. I was trying to cut on the bass drum and make splices. I said to him, "I'm having a rough time hearing the kick drum under the speakers like this." He responded, "Well, that's because your shirt is too loud." [*laughs*]

As you look back on the significance of the album three decades later, how do you feel about Prince and being involved in the making of such a compelling album?

David Z: I've been involved with a few hits, but when a song gets so big, it is something you never expect to happen, especially after the conversation I had over the song "Kiss." I never thought it would have such a *huge* impact on music. But it did. It's almost like, when you hear the song playing on the radio or in the club, you're like, "I didn't have anything to do with that." [*laughs*] You take a step back and say what the hell. The power of the media made everyone aware of it. That's what was amazing to me was the power of the media. When you create a song, you're doing it for yourself. Making music is something we do for ourselves as musicians. If it makes us happy, then that's great. Luckily, it coincides with the public's taste. It's amazing how everyone gets inundated with your song and the power of the media was fantastic. Whenever I'd work on something, I'd always think about what Prince would think. He was the guy I compared everything to. His opinion on things was my beacon of goodness. I really miss him.

Susan Rogers: The outpouring of attention, respect, and affection that we've seen after his passing is something I never would've imagined in my wildest dreams. What he received in public adoration is what I thought he deserved. I wished he would've had more of that during his lifetime. I'm very grateful to see that the public is recognizing what an important figure he was in American music. I was grateful then and aware of how lucky I was every minute [of] every day to be working with that guy. It was not lost on me at all. I was a fan of his before I began working for him. I believed he was great very early on. To look back on it now, I think the public got this one right. There is no mistake in recognizing the importance and brilliance of this American musician. He is dearly missed by all of us. ❍

(*opposite*) Photograph by Jeff Katz. Courtesy of Warner Bros.

Singer and Prince protegé JILL JONES spent five years working on her debut album for Paisley Park. With the help of producer David Z and Prince himself, Jones created a perfect pop album and a wildly creative work of art—but it unfortunately went underheard and underappreciated in its time.

POP ART

by Michael A. Gonzales

The musical/visual landscape of the 1980s overflowed with the power of so-called divas blaring from Top 40 radio, telegenic profiling in video clips on MTV, and glamorously strutting on concert stages throughout the world. While Detroit homegirl Madonna usually receives credit for igniting the post-disco inferno of provocative pop, documentarians of the era often overlook the aural contributions of high-heeled groundbreakers Vanity 6. Developed by Prince in mid-1981, the group featured exotic lead vocalist Denise Matthews (Vanity) singing alongside Brenda Bennett and Susan Moonsie. Clad in lingerie, panty hose, and garter belts, the sexy trio's self-titled debut album, which featured the smoldering funk/new-wave single "Nasty Girl," was the template for the times that sonically (and visually) inspired a decade of future sensations that included Madonna, Lisa Lisa, Janet Jackson, Pebbles, Jody Watley, and so many others.

While Vanity 6 was the songwriter/producer's first foray into crafting female-driven pop hits in the tradition of Phil Spector, Holland-Dozier-Holland, and Curtis Mayfield, it was just the beginning of a long career of Prince's collaboration with women artists. By the mid-'80s, in addition to his own brilliant albums and singles, Prince's wondrous tracks with women artists included platinum hits with Shelia E. ("The Glamorous Life"), the Bangles ("Manic Monday"), and Sheena Easton ("Sugar Walls"), each with Prince credited under a different pseudonym. However, for many fans of the music Prince created during that electric era, the best album of the Paisley period was made by a former small-town-Ohio girl turned California teen Jill Jones, an attractive, fair-skinned, biracial sister with long brown hair, intriguing eyes, and a baby face, whose self-titled masterwork was released to little fanfare in 1987.

A timeless record that still sounds as though it were recorded tomorrow, *Jill Jones* (Paisley Park) was a long labor of love and talent

that the singer recorded over five years with producers Prince and David Z. Engineer Susan Rogers, who worked with Jones on many sessions, once called her the most patient artist signed to Paisley Park—whose roster included the Family, Mazarati, Taja Sevelle, and Madhouse—since it took five years from her first joining the camp for her album to come out.

"In the beginning, I wasn't really there to record an album," Jill Jones says from her home in Los Angeles; born in 1962, she was four years younger than Prince. "I moved [to Minneapolis] in 1982, but I didn't sign a recording contract with Paisley until 1986. I came to Minneapolis because Prince explained his vision of Paisley to me, and I believed in it. With his artists, it was more than music; Prince was trying to start a movement."

Nearly thirty years after the release of *Jill Jones*, former SoulTrain. com editor and singer Rhonda Nicole can still remember the thrill of buying the cassette at a local *wrecka stow* in New Orleans while visiting her grandparents: "I was a preteen girl, so I loved the pink tint on the cover photo, but I was also studying music and playing saxophone, so I was impressed by the strings and horns. I loved Jill's voice on that album, because she had an assertiveness you don't hear in other Prince-produced artists. Her screams on 'All Day, All Night' were so wild and powerful. Listening to her vocals on the dreamy 'Violet Blue,' I appreciated that her voice was more raw than pretty, but she still sounded cool. The entire *Jill Jones* album was lush, dramatic, romantic, and outrageous, and it still holds up decades later."

After breaking with Paisley Park in 1990, Jill Jones, whose last album, *I Am* (Peace Bisquit), was released in 2016, toured with Chic and recorded with Ryuichi Sakamoto ("You Do Me"). Still, although she made only one album with Prince, that eight-song disc was brilliant enough to turn her into an iconic cult singer whose long out-of-print debut still commands respect. "Prince worked on so many side-projects where the music was great, but the singers were just lackluster," Alex Hahn, co-author of *The Rise of Prince: 1958–1988*, says. "Jill Jones's record was different, because she had so much more personality and vitality than Vanity or Sheena Easton, and it all came through in her music."

When I spoke to Jones seven months after Prince's sudden death on April 21, 2016, she was still coming to grips with losing her friend, former lover, and yesteryear employer for whom she also once served as a muse; but still I got a sense of that bubbly, slightly kooky character that came across on her debut. "Many years had gone by since Prince and I last saw each other, but I'm glad I got to see him before he passed," she says. "It was after Vanity's memorial service, and it was me, Apollonia, and Susan Moonsie. He looked frail, but he was still cracking jokes. I thought we would be cracking jokes for a long time, but it didn't work out that way."

Jill Jones first met Prince in late 1980 at eighteen when she was singing backgrounds on tour with family friend, adopted big sister, and "white chocolate" soul singer Teena Marie. It wasn't her voice that first caught Prince's attention but her mouth. "We were in Buffalo, New York, opening on the *Dirty Mind* tour," Jones says. "Our sound check was too close to the opening of the show, and the stage was too small. Teena and I passed him in the hall, and someone introduced them. I just looked at him and smirked, saying some smart-aleck remark about the stage. I was a bratty eighteen-year-old kid, but my attitude got his attention."

Like many horny-toad boys in the summer of 1984 who sat through repeated viewings of *Purple Rain*, I'd fallen in love with Jill Jones who played the constantly dissed waitress who was obviously in love with the Kid. Rarely smiling, she was sexy and mysterious as a mixed Holly Golightly. It was only later that I realized that she was also the blond sex kitten behind the keyboards with Lisa Coleman in the "1999" video as well one of the voices heard on the 1982 album.

Credited as J.J. in the liner notes of *1999*, Jones provided backing vocals on the title track single as well as "Automatic," "Free," and "Lady Cab Driver." But, why the initials instead of her full name? "Prince liked to have an air of mystery," Jones responds, "so when I asked him why he put J.J. instead of my name, he said, 'Let the fans wonder who you are.' He just didn't want to put the whole name out there yet."

After the release of *1999* in October 1982, Jill Jones became a fixture on Prince's recordings, providing backing vocals for Apollonia 6 ("Ooo She She Wa Wa"), Sheila E. ("The Belle of St. Mark"), the Time (*Pandemonium*), and Mazarati ("Strawberry Lover"), just to name a few. "Sometimes, I didn't even know what songs I was doing backgrounds for, because he would add different parts to different mixes. At that time, Prince liked background vocals that weren't all soul-sister screams."

Jill hadn't planned on being molded by Prince, but one night while watching a Marilyn Monroe movie, he decided to cut her hair and dye it blond. "Prince said I looked like every girl with long brown hair and I needed something to stand out. He said, 'When Vanity walks in a room, people know she's a star. You need your own thing.' He took me in the bathroom and cut my hair with fingernail scissors. He did a really good job. Prince always said if he hadn't been a musician, he might've become a hairdresser."

Before Jones appeared in front of the cameras for the "1999" video, Prince also sexed up her image, forcing her to part with the jeans and Ralph Lauren sweaters that were a staple of her wardrobe. Jill Jones was being Svengalied by the best, but she stopped the process cold when Prince wanted to change her name to Elektra: "Prince was a big fan of the [Frank Miller–created comic book character] Elektra and had written a song called 'Come Elektra Tuesday' that he wanted me to sing. His manager Steve Fargnoli came to my rescue and told Prince I was already established as a singer, so I didn't have to change my name."

Between recordings, hairstyling, and wardrobe changes, Prince and Jill spent a lot of time watching movies. Jones says, "We saw *Swept Away*, lots of Fellini films, [classic musicals from choreographer] Busby Berkeley, and David Lynch's *Eraserhead*. I can remember us both being grossed out by the baby scene." When it came time to make his own film debut, *Purple Rain*, he had originally planned to make Jones's part larger and give her a musical number ("Wednesday"), but neither happened. "I didn't really care, because I wasn't trying to be famous, because all of that was a little scary to me. It mattered more that he thought I was a good actress. I laughed when he told me that and said, 'Maybe in this room I am.' He was so excited during that time while also trying to learn about filmmaking. I'd see him talking to the DP or talking to [*Purple Rain* director] Albert Magnoli, because he seriously wanted to learn the process."

It was during this purple period that Jill also became friendly with Prince's father, John L. Nelson, a former jazz pianist who collaborated with his boy on the *Purple Rain* tracks as well as the title track for the next year's *Around the World in a Day*. "Prince's music started to change when John L. came into the fold," Jones says. "Prince's dad could play the most intricate chord structures, and Prince started working on his chops more. It was nice to see them together. Prince was very generous with his father, offering him support and pushing his dad to do new music. At the same time, John L.'s presence pushed Prince as well: he practiced more and started including beautiful orchestrations and Clare Fischer strings."

Although much of Prince's newfound musical moxie and artful arrangements were poured into *Around the World in a Day* and *Parade*, a lot of that vibe spilled over into *Jill Jones*. For her part in the process, Jones brought a wealth of craft, dedication, and personal experience to the project. In fact, and she'd been waiting to shine as a soloist for a long time.

Jill Jones was being raised in Ohio by her grandparents, but when she turned twelve, she moved to Los Angeles to be with her mother, who had been working as a model. This journey to the West Coast definitely came with its perks, as her stepfather was Fuller Gordy, the eldest brother of Motown mogul Berry. The iconic soul label had boarded up its Detroit headquarters and studio and headed west in 1972. Fuller Gordy was in charge of administration, dealing with personnel and company policy, and Jill's mother, Winnie Jones, began managing young acts, including Rick James and Teena Marie.

Jill went to Beverly Hills High School where a younger classmate named Lenny Kravitz used to trail her around the halls. "Lenny was a few years younger than me," Jones recalls, "and all the girls loved him. But he had a crush on me and would follow me everywhere." Once, when Lenny had run away from home, it was Teena Marie who helped him, cooking for him and facilitating his musical pursuits while he continued to attend Beverly Hills High. Meanwhile, after school, Jones usually headed to the L.A. Motown offices located at 6255 Sunset Tower between Vine and Argyle.

"My house was up a big hill, so instead of climbing that to go home, I'd go there," she recalls. "I saw everybody up there. Diana Ross, Marvin Gaye, and Smokey Robinson were always there. Berry used to have these large Motown family events at his house, and everybody was invited to compete in these tournaments. One year, it was chess; another year, it was backgammon that was the rage. Sometimes, I

Artist: Jill Jones
Album: *Jill Jones*
Label: Paisley Park
Release year: 1987
Produced by: David Z and Jill Jones
Co-produced by: Prince (three songs)
Written by: Jill Jones and Prince
Engineered by: Coke Johnson, Susan Rogers, Peggy McCreary
Recorded at: Paisley Park and Electric Lady (New York)
Orchestra arranged and conducted by: Clare Fischer

played, but other times, I'd just sit with [Berry's father] Pops Gordy and listen to his stories. With the Gordy empire, there was a real sense of self-love and achievement that couldn't help but be passed down to me."

Jill also started accompanying her aunt Iris Gordy to the studio with then-rising Motown artist Tata Vega, who in 1975 was working on her debut, *Full Speed Ahead*. "Motown was hoping that Tata, who had a powerhouse style, would rival Chaka Khan," Jones says. "She had a great, inspiring voice. I started doing my first background singing on a few of her tracks when I was thirteen."

However, after Jill's mother began working with Teena Marie—who was originally the lead singer in a group called Kryptonite (later rechristened Apollo) with Berry Gordy's son Kerry and future mega manager Benny Medina—young Jill started spending more time with her. Teena, eight years older than Jill, became like an older sister and eventually wound up living with the family. "Teena used to drive me to school in the mornings and pick me up in the afternoon," Jill says. "There was a White girl that tried to jump me, and when I told Teena, she came up to school and went all Venice gang member on her. She was my protector, my best friend, and my mentor. Teena opened up my world. I spent countless hours riding in the car with her, listening to the Beatles and Led Zeppelin, or going surfing. When she took the Kryptonite gig, I'd go to rehearsals with her, but, truthfully, it wasn't a good fit and Teena was miserable. For me, I loved being with her and having these experiences I never would've had if I stayed in Ohio."

With Teena unhappy, Winnie and Iris Gordy connected her with the label's latest star (and soon-to-be Prince rival) Rick James, whose glittering grit-raw debut, *Come Get It* (1978), was street-corner hard, dance-floor ready, and included the classic weed track "Mary Jane." At first, Rick was hesitant, wanting to work only on his own material, but after hearing Teena rehearsing at the Motown office, he relented and the two began working together on her debut, *Wild and Peaceful*, which featured the James-penned single "I'm a Sucker for Your Love." Years later, Marie told an interviewer, "I was a gift to him and he was a gift to me."

While fifteen-year-old Jill attended a few of the recording sessions, she also started showing up at the band's house with her school friends instead of going to class. "Rick had a house in Coldwater Canyon and I would come by at ten in the morning," Jill says, laughing. "I only let my friends come so I could use their cars. The Stone City Band backing vocalist [and percussionist] Jackie [Ruffin] would let us in. She would be half asleep, but always so nice. Her husband, [keyboardist] Levi [Ruffin Jr.], would be there and they might make breakfast. Rick would come downstairs, rubbing his eyes, and ask, 'Don't y'all have school?' I would tell him that I didn't have any early morning classes. Finally, Rick called my mom. He ratted me out so bad that my mom went to the principal's office to find the fake notes I'd written. I got in so much trouble; I was so mad." That same year, Jill started co-writing with Teena [for "The Ballad of Cradle Rob and Me"] and providing backing vocals during her recording sessions.

The following year, when Jill turned sweet sixteen, Rick James gifted her with a beautiful necklace for her birthday. Although Rick was a notorious wild boy, he usually tried to act right around Jill. "But there was that one time I was in the studio and almost knocked over this mound of cocaine that was on the table, and everybody in the room started going nuts," Jill says. "Seeing everybody's reaction made me never want to experiment with coke. I had never seen such craziness in my life."

Years later, when Jill started hanging out with Prince publicly, the two ran into Rick James one night at Carlos'n Charlie's. "The rivalry between them was very real, so when Rick saw me, he asked real loud where my sweet-sixteen necklace was. I was mortified; I just wanted

to turn to dust, because I felt as though he was treating me like a little girl. I said, 'I'm not sixteen anymore, Rick, you better calm down. He came over to me and said, 'And look who you're hanging out with.' There was no love lost between those guys."

In 1980, when Teena's second album, *Irons in the Fire*, was released, she was invited to open for Prince's tour. Previously, they'd been doing little club gigs as well as a short-run opening for Shaun Cassidy. "That was funny," says Jones, "because the audience was filled with little girls and we were dressed in these tight, sexy clothes. We played in Utah and Colorado, but that wasn't our audience. Finally, we went out on the road with Rick, and then we jumped on Prince's tour."

For Teena, it was a dream gig, but Jill was content playing it cool. "One day, Prince and Teena were in the same hotel, and he came over to me and said, 'I heard your voice through the soundboard. It's really good.' We started talking and he was really funny, but everything he said I had a clap-back for it. Back then, I was the clap-back queen." Prince played his mack-daddy part with heart, but he also began spreading fake news about Jill to keep his homeboy/bassist André Cymone at bay. According to Jill, "André approached me one night and asked, 'Are you married?' When I started laughing, he said, 'Prince told me you were married.' After that, he became like my big brother on the tour."

Cymone, on the other hand, remembered the situation somewhat differently. "Jill and I were friendly, but the problem for me was, I knew her mom and Teena to a certain degree," Dre says. "Both were very sweet women. But I was such a scoundrel back then, and I didn't want to get in trouble with them." Prince also told her the funny tale of Cymone bringing his boom box on the road because he thought he'd be able to pick up Minneapolis radio station KMOJ even when he wasn't in the right city. "Prince wouldn't let me live that down."

After the tour was over, Jill and Prince stayed in touch, but two years passed before they would collaborate on music when he asked her to contribute vocals to the synth-funk masterwork *1999*. Moving to Minneapolis in 1982, she lived with Prince and hung out with him steady. "He loved driving around town, blaring music in the car," Jill recalls. "He'd play the Cocteau Twins, Miles Davis, Jimi Hendrix, Nino Rota, Roxy Music's *Avalon* album. He once made me a mixtape with nothing but Miles Davis songs on it." Jones also had to get used to Prince's nocturnal ways. "The night we recorded '1999,' I was in bed, and he woke me up in the middle of the night. We lived in Chanhassen, but Lisa drove in as well and sang with me." When Prince traveled to Cali to record parts of *1999* at Sunset Sound, Jill would be there too. And when Prince was finished with his stuff, he'd start working on hers.

Five years later, when *Jill Jones* was finally in stores, it was doomed from the beginning. When her feisty yet sexually charged first single "Mia Bocca" was released, there was resistance from MTV to play the video in prime time. "We had that crazy bitch Tipper Gore going after us with her Parents Music Resource Center [PMRC] that was trying to censor music based on sexual content," Jones says. "MTV would only play it at certain times at night."

Directed by French photographer and music-video director Jean-Baptiste Mondino, who later shot the *Lovesexy* album cover, the sepia-tinted clip was reminiscent of Fellini films and though sexy, still innocent. "Prince had nothing to do with the video," Jones says. "I just went to Mexico with the director and the production team. Prince spared no expense and he loved it; he said it captured the essence of me."

Meanwhile, the people at radio kept trying to leverage with Paisley Park, telling them they'd only play his artists if Prince did a concert

---

(*opposite*) Original Jill Jones press photo by Isabel Snyder for Paisley Park.

Jill Jones in the 1984 film *Purple Rain*.

for their corporate such and such. "Prince had such high hopes for Paisley Park," says Jones. "But, unfortunately, it never manifested the way he wanted. They kept trying to compromise him, and wouldn't allow him to run the business as a business. They just swarmed and compromised him."

Prince's trusted studio companion David Z, one of the few to receive actual production credit, worked on the album as well. According to Jones, "Prince trusted David to articulate what he wanted. Prince might fly in when I was working on vocals, but many nights it was just me and David at Electric Lady. Prince was filming *Under a Cherry Moon*, so he gave us a ton of freedom." Writer Miles Marshall Lewis, currently working on the book *Paisley Park Forever*, says, "At the time, his role was to polish up tracks Prince handed him for Paisley Park acts like Mazarati, who he also coproduced. On *Jill Jones*, David did five of the eight songs, but Prince coproduced 'Mia Bocca,' 'For Love,' and 'All Day, All Night' himself."

The second single was the raunchy dance track "G-Spot." While the song, with its prominent honking saxophone, was supposedly written for Vanity 6, Jill says, "I was there when Prince did the demo for 'G-Spot.' I was reading an article about it and we talked about it on the plane. On the demo, Prince played the sax part himself. I didn't even know he could play, but if Prince had to wait too long for something, he just did it himself. Later, he would bring in other players, but he knew the lines that he wanted. I loved working with him in the studio, because he knew everything there was to know

about it. If something went wrong, he knew how to crawl under the board and fix it."

For me, the standout on Jill Jones was the jazzy pop fusion of "Violet Blue," a lyric that began as an entry in the singer's journal. "Around the time Prince and his dad went to meet Elizabeth Taylor, and I remember they kept talking about her eyes, which were violet blue. It's a song about choices and decisions. It was around that time that he got engaged to Susannah Melvoin."

The fem-funk of "For Love" was the last single released but, like the previous two, failed to chart. Although Prince and Jill Jones started working on a second album, the project fell apart. "It became difficult to do a second record with him, because we were not approaching it the same way," Jones recalls. "He was putting more pressure on me, and it just wasn't working between us anymore." After her appearance in the horrid *Graffiti Bridge* movie, where her part had been sliced considerably before filming, Jill Jones stepped away from the Paisley wonderland and did her own thing.

Although there was very little written about *Jill Jones* in the American music press in 1987 (the album was better received in Europe), Prince biographer Dave Hill spoke for us who loved it when he wrote in his book *Pop Life*, "Jill Jones is the female Prince protégé who sounded most like herself." Thirty years later, the record remains the best album released bearing the Paisley Park label. "I loved that project so much," Jones says. "To me, it was like a work of art." ◗

Prince's trusted engineer Susan Rogers speaks at length about his sprawling epic, SIGN "O" THE TIMES, which was recorded between 1986 and 1987—with other, older tracks pulled from the vaults—a record ultimately created from the ashes of the aborted albums *Camille*, *Dream Factory*, and *Crystal Ball*.

THE EPIC

by Chris Williams

From your point of view, what was Prince's mind-set going into the creation of *Sign "O" the Times* after his *Parade* album a year prior?

Susan Rogers: Well, I really didn't know what he was thinking, because he tended to not reveal that kind of stuff. I'm assuming that he was proud of the *Parade* record and the movie. The album was well received, and "Girls & Boys" and "Kiss" were hit singles, so I think his personal outlook was very positive and optimistic, and musically he was looking for the next new thing, meaning new things he could say and new ways he could express a groove, melodies, tonalities, and timbres. These were things he didn't express on his previous record. His mood was generally like it always was. He was serious, pensive, upbeat, and optimistic. He was a thoughtful person. Things were changing around the camp then. Wendy, Lisa, and Bobby Z. were the heart of the Revolution. Wendy and Lisa were aching to get out there on their own and to express themselves musically. I think Prince was thinking that now would be a good time to make a change. The general consensus within the camp was that this train was going to keep on rolling. It was a mutual decision when Wendy and Lisa decided to leave. His mood and approach was to try something different and to see what he could do. Susannah Melvoin, Wendy's twin sister, was still around, so that connection was still there to Wendy and Lisa. It caused a little bit of tension, and naturally it would, because Susannah was missing Wendy, and Wendy was missing Susannah. They were really close. Because of that tension, it fueled a creative atmosphere.

It was a funny time to be working with him without Wendy and Lisa. The sorrow of their absence was also felt in the room. The imminent departure of Susannah was coming, because she wasn't happy, and he wasn't happy either. They were engaged to be married, but it became clear to them that it wasn't going to happen. So they broke off the engagement. *Sign "O" the Times* represented Prince soldiering through a tough time, personally and professionally. There were changes, and it's hard for people to cope with changes. As an artist, he coped with them by pushing forward and writing his way through it. That can go either way—it can yield some of the best work you'll ever do, or it can yield work that is self-indulgent, dispirited, and apathetic. In this case, it yielded some of his very best work.

Sign "O" the Times **resulted from a combination of three different albums that Prince was working on:** *Camille*, *Dream Factory*, **and** *Crystal Ball*. **What was Prince's overall creative approach during this time?**

When we came off the *Parade* tour [which wrapped up in September 1986], Prince was constantly recording; and as he was recording, sometimes in the arc of that constant process, he would pull tracks together with a concept for an album. *Crystal Ball* and *Dream Factory* were both emerging around that time. He was playing around with certain ideas: Will there be another version of the Time? Will there be another band that will be an alter ego that will handle certain kinds of tracks? He had this character called Camille. He wanted to try some new stuff. It's what any artist does when they're going fishing for a perspective or concept for their next record. At one point, the album that became *Sign "O" the Times* was a three-record set. While in discussions with Warner Bros., his record label at the time, they were absolutely unwilling to release a three-record set, because it would've been too expensive to manufacture and the profit margin wouldn't have been as high. I can say from personal observation that Prince was unhappy about that decision. He wanted that three-record set, but push was coming to shove at that point. So he regrouped and he came

Photograph by Jeff Katz, originally shot for the inner sleeve of *Sign "O" the Times*. Courtesy of Warner Bros.

up with a perspective and vision for his next album. It was darker in tone than the *Parade* record and much darker in tone than *Around the World in a Day*. I'd say even darker in tone than his *Purple Rain* record, because this time he was talking about world affairs.

The song "Sign 'O' the Times" was about how things were changing in the United States and in the world with AIDS. In the United States, there was gang warfare and poverty. There were things changing with Prince too. His band was changing and his musical style wasn't as popular as it had once been. Funk dance music was getting the elbow from hip-hop, because hip-hop was coming up through the pop charts. It became clear that a new sheriff was in town [*laughs*]—this sheriff was hip-hop—and that it was going to rule. It was abundantly clear, and Prince was smart enough to know what was coming. He was also smart enough to recognize that musical styles change. It doesn't matter how great you are. James Brown's style went out of favor, the Beatles' style went out of favor, and the big arena rock of Led Zeppelin went out of favor, so you can kind of predict that it's going to happen to you too. It will happen pretty fast in the music business. This is what helped give *Sign "O" the Times* its somber tone.

When did you begin the recording sessions for *Sign "O" the Times*?

It didn't have a definitive start date like most people's albums do. Most people will plan an album, get together with a producer, do preproduction and work out arrangements, book studio time, and go in and make a record. But Prince wasn't like that. He didn't work like that. Prince recorded *constantly*. So things that were coming into fruition may or may not be part of a record. For example, the song "Sign 'O' the Times" was recorded when he was in a burst of recording and writing. "Play in the Sunshine" was one of the songs that came along at the very end. "Play in the Sunshine" was really written just to be a segue song to take us from "Sign 'O' the Times" into "Housequake." It was like a tomato on a sandwich. It complemented the meat and cheese. The main songs of this record were "Sign 'O' the Times," "Housequake," "U Got the Look," "If I Was Your Girlfriend," "Strange Relationship," "The Cross," and "Adore." Some of the other songs were pulled out of the vault. "I Could Never Take the Place of Your Man" preceded 1983; it was an old song. He had me pull that out of the vault so that we could continue working on it by making some changes and then putting it on the record. "It's Gonna Be a Beautiful Night" was recorded with the Revolution live, when we were in Paris. "Slow Love" was another *really* old song. It was an old one from the vault. It wasn't a serial, chronological process. There was some old material and brand-new material that complemented those core songs.

Take me through the different studio setups.

He liked working at home and at Sunset Sound Studios [in Los Angeles, California]. At this point, Paisley Park Studios was in its final stages of being built. This was in late 1986 and early 1987. Prince's options were to record at his home studio on Galpin Boulevard in Chanhassen, Minnesota. It was just up the street from Paisley Park. It was a really nice home, and there was a basement studio that had a large control room and a medium-sized isolation booth right next to it. The piano was upstairs and it was used for smaller projects. We tried to fit the whole band in there once, but it wasn't big enough for a band. He recorded songs like "The Ballad of Dorothy Parker" at home. We did "Hot Thing," "Forever in My Life," and "It" there. The other songs were done at Sunset Sound Studios in Studio 3. It was his favorite studio in the world. We did "Sign 'O' the Times," "Play in the Sunshine," "Housequake," "U Got the Look," "Adore,"

and "The Cross" there. When we worked at Sunset Sound, it was a big enough room that we could have everything set up all at once. The piano could always be miked, the B-3 organ could be miked and ready and go, drum kit could be set up and ready to go, and he would have his keyboard, bass, and guitars with him in the control room. Because I was his employee, I would be out there working with him engineering these sessions along with Peggy McCreary. Peggy had been an assistant engineer at Sunset Sound for quite a few years, and he liked working with Peggy when she was around. I believe Coke Johnson worked with us on a few of those sessions as well.

The way we would work is, that stuff would be miked all the time. Prince would often come in with lyrics already written, not always but often, usually for ballads. He'd either program the drum machine right there in the control room, or he'd go out and play live drums. If he was playing live drums or programming the drum machine, he had the song basically in his head. He knew where the breaks were, so he'd play an intro, then he'd do a fill that would go into a verse, or he'd play the verse for eight bars, then he'd do a breakdown or a fill that would get us into a chorus. He knew where to put the cymbals at, because he already had the arrangement in his head. After we finished recording the drums, we'd hand him the bass and he'd put on the bass part and he'd put on the basic keyboard and guitar parts. Usually, midway through a song is when he would stop and do vocals. He liked to do vocals alone in the control room, so we'd set up the vocal mic for him. He'd have a patch cord with a piece of tape on it that represented his signal for that vocal mic, and all he had to do was to move it to different tracks after doing a lead, if he wanted to do background vocals. So he did his vocals by himself, then Peggy and I would come back in the room and finish it up by adding the remaining overdubs and getting the song mixed as we went along to then print it and be done for the night. Some songs took a *long* time. One in particular was "U Got the Look." "U Got the Look" went through a lot of different permutations. He tried it at different tempos and tried it with different feels. It was unusual for him, but he really liked the track. I think he was feeling like this song was going to be a single. He brought in Sheena Easton at some point. I don't believe for a minute that it was planned from the beginning. It was just that she was around at the time. We spent three or four days on "U Got the Look," which was unusual for him.

What was the typical studio routine for you and Prince throughout this recording process?

Like a lot of artists, he'd be up all night. The general modus operandi was we would start, either in the late morning or early afternoon, because in the mornings, is when he would take care of business or any managerial issues he had to deal with. Once he began working in the studio, he didn't like to stop or be interrupted. So let's say we started at noon, we'd walk out of there certainly after the sun was up. We'd walk out at nine or ten o'clock in the morning, then we'd sleep for a few hours and resume things again. It was kind of a rotating clock. We rarely started at night, at least not late at night, but it wasn't unheard of to start at six or seven o'clock in the evening then work all night. His dial was constantly rotating. I could expect an eighteen, twenty, or twenty-four hour workday. It was fairly common to work a forty-eight hour session. It was very common to work a twenty-four hour session. When we were working on "U Got the Look," it just took *days* and *days* to finish it. I remember, at one point, looking at my watch and I thought it said nine o'clock. I wondered if it was nine o'clock in the morning or nine o'clock at night. When I was staring at my watch, I noticed it was upside down, so then I wondered if it was three o'clock in the morning or three o'clock in the afternoon. [*laughs*]

Artist: Prince
Album: *Sign "O" the Times*
Label: Paisley Park
Release year: 1987
Performed, produced, arranged, and composed by: Prince ("Starfish and Coffee" lyrics co-written by Susannah Melvoin; "Slow Love" lyrics co-written by Carol Davis; "It's Gonna Be a Beautiful Night" music co-written by Dr. Fink and Eric Leeds)
Engineered by: Susan Rogers, Coke Johnson, and Prince
Recorded and mixed at: Paisley Park, Sunset Sound, and Dierks Studio Mobile Trucks
Mastered by: Bernie Grundman

Saxophone: Eric Leeds
Trumpet: Atlanta Bliss
Drums, percussion, and rap: Sheila E.
Backing and additional lead vocals: Susannah Melvoin, Lisa Melvoin, Sheena Easton, Greg Brooks, Jerome Benton, Wally Safford, and Jill Jones
Strings arrangement: Clare Fischer
Additional guitar, tambourine, and congas: Wendy Melvoin
Sitar and wooden flute: Lisa Coleman
Lead guitar: Miko Weaver
Additional performance by: The Revolution
Cover photo by: Jeff Katz

When we were working at Sunset Sound, there wasn't any windows. It was fully contained. There was a lounge and a bathroom, so you could go for days without ever walking outside, if you needed to, and you wouldn't know if it was day or night because you were that exhausted and the hours flew by. To work with someone who was never on drugs, lazy, or disrespectful, was a great thing. He had a workingman's attitude toward the work we were doing in the studio. We were constantly being productive. Things were getting done and made. It was an exciting environment where we were watching creative work come together, and I was participating in that process. It was thrilling to be working with him at that time. It was more than enough reason to stay awake. There were no complaints from me. [*laughs*] Eric Leeds and Matt Blistan [aka Atlanta Bliss] would come to the studio to play saxophone and trumpet. Susannah Melvoin would do some backing vocals, and she was in the studio a lot. Sheila E. would play percussion on some of the songs. For the most part, this album was all Prince.

Where were you positioned in the studio in relation to Prince?

Well, if he was doing acoustic drums, acoustic piano, or B-3 organ, he'd be on the other side of the glass. For everything else, he was right next to me. [*laughs*] I was sitting behind the console routing the signal, and he was sitting next to me playing bass or keys. We were right next to each other for most of four years. I was with him on tour, because he liked to record wherever he was.

Did he do any demos for the songs on this album?

No. Not at all. He was unusual compared to other artists. A lot of artists will do demos just to live with it before they commit the arrangement to tape. Prince worked so fast that he wouldn't waste his time demoing. There were two exceptions for this album though. "Strange Relationship" was a song that the band worked out at rehearsal a lot. He tried a lot of different arrangements at rehearsal. So it really wasn't demoing in the way we think about demoing. This song was a rare exception. It had been around for a long time. Sometimes, he would pull out old material and redo it. In the case of "Slow Love" and "I Could Never Take the Place of Your Man," those weren't substantially redone from how they were originally stored back in 1982. He basically updated them, and we mixed them.

What were the names of the instruments and equipment you used to capture the sounds for the songs on this album?

When I was working with him, he loved his Linn LM-1 drum machine. It was the early model that preceded the more popular LinnDrum. At home, he had a Yamaha piano. He liked the Yamaha drums as well. On this record, he used the Fairlight CMI, which was a very sophisticated synthesizer. He used it *a lot*. The only people who could afford it had a large amount of money. I would say the Fairlight was the sound for the *Sign "O" the Times* record. He was still using his Yamaha DX7. He liked that synthesizer. He wasn't using his earlier stuff like the Oberheim synthesizer. The Oberheim synthesizer sound defined his *Controversy*, *1999*, and *Purple Rain* albums. Those albums had a bright, robust, harsh tone. They had a really nice rock-and-roll tone, but he was abandoning those at this point, in favor of the softer tones of the Fairlight and DX7. He was probably tired of the Oberheim. He was still using his same guitar, the Hohner Telecaster. The bass guitars were still the same.

Sheila E., Prince, and Cat.
Promotional photo for the concert film *Sign "O" the Times*.

(*opposite*) Cat and Sheila E. (*above*) Prince in concert. Promotional photos for the concert film *Sign "O" the Times*.

Sheila E. on drums. Promotional photo for the concert film *Sign "O" the Times*.

Earlier you mentioned that he liked to record his lead vocals alone. Did he record his background vocals in a similar fashion?

If he was singing background vocals, he'd sing them alone. If it was going to be Wendy, Lisa, Susannah, or Jill Jones doing the background vocals, he'd leave the studio and let us do it on our own. He would leave me alone to do horn arrangements with Eric Leeds as well. He'd tell Eric, "Take it away! Do what you like." Prince would go to dinner or on a date or to the club, then when he would come back, we'd finish his parts. He was a genius with those backing-vocal arrangements. He really loved those gospel chords. He loved sevenths, ninths, and thirteenths. He was *so great* at it. He was quick with layering harmonies. It didn't take him any time at all. He was brilliant at everything he ever did. He'd always say, "We're going to go to church on this one." [*laughs*] On this record, I can think of one exception where he wasn't especially brilliant, and that was during the making of "The Cross." The drums on "The Cross" weren't steady; they were sped up. I thought for sure he was going to redo the drums on it, because he played the drums on it all in one take and it just progressively became faster. It really bugged me, because I thought it was sloppy. I was hoping that he'd redo it, but he was satisfied with it, and he knew what he was doing, so who was I to argue. It was one instance where I thought he could've tightened something up. [*laughs*]

Can you take me through the mixing process for the songs on the album?

The mixing process happened as the songs were being overdubbed. The way most artists do it is they finish the final overdubs and they put the tape away, then they give it to a mixing engineer. The mixing engineer starts from scratch by combining these sounds to turn the collection of tracks into a vinyl record. But Prince didn't do it this way. He didn't want to put the tape away until it was *done, done, done.* So I would be getting sounds when he was doing the last of the overdubs. We would be tweaking the mix as we went along, then all that remained was a few hours of work. We'd polish it up a little bit, then print it. Mixing is kind of like an arrangement. Our mixing process was concurrent with the recording process, unless there was a problem. If there was a problem, we spent a lot of time mixing it. If it wasn't coming together, the song would probably end up in the vault, or in the case of "U Got the Look," the song was too good to go in the vault. He started to change things. I remember changing the speed on "U Got the Look" and totally redoing it. At some point, we made it much slower, and at another point, we made it much faster, until we got the final groove that he was happy with.

When the album was being constructed, were there any interesting behind-the-scenes stories that took place?

One thing I can say that was interesting is on the song "Forever in My Life." Prince somehow got off sync, because he was monitoring the track himself when he was doing his lead and backing vocals. When he was doing his backing vocals, he opted to do his backing vocals first and he came in on the wrong bar of the intro. This is why it kind of sounds like a little bit of a round. I haven't listened to the song in a long time, but I think the backing vocals precede the lead vocals by like four bars. He was happy with it, even though it was an accident. He was excited by it.

"Starfish and Coffee" was about Susannah [Melvoin] telling him a story about a girl [Cynthia Rose] that she went to school with that was cognitively impaired. Prince just loved that story. With Susannah, he wrote lyrics about it. On this track, we used the backwards drums, which entailed recording the arrangement backwards, so we recorded the drums and flipped the tape upside down and overdubbed it from there on out. So that was kind of fun as well.

Did Prince ever mention any artists from this era being his direct competition, or was he completely focused on making his music the best it could possibly be?

I think he was aware of and promoted a healthy rivalry between himself and Michael Jackson. He didn't talk about any other artists that were his direct competition other than Michael Jackson. He was aware of what Jackson was doing. I don't think he saw himself having to pass a test of who was better or who was worst because they were two different kinds of musicians. But he was aware that Michael Jackson had things that he would never have. The public adored Michael Jackson. Michael Jackson was considered the kid next door that you would love to have as your neighbor or dating your daughter. He had this squeaky, wholesome image. Prince was kind of the scary guy. The guy you didn't want your daughter dating. He might be trouble.

One time, one of the guys at Sunset Sound told me, "The reason why I like Bruce Springsteen better than Prince is because I think Bruce Springsteen would sit down and have a beer with me, and I'm afraid that Prince would steal my girlfriend." I didn't know Bruce Springsteen, but I knew Prince. Prince would never steal anybody's girlfriend. If you knew him, you would want your daughter to date him. He was respectful and squeaky clean. We used to make jokes about how he would get high off of Coca-Cola, because he didn't use profanity or drugs. He was as sober as a judge. He was such a respectable fellow. He saw himself in musical competition with Michael [Jackson]. Madonna was kind of sniffing around. Madonna wanted to be like him, but he didn't want to be like her. He didn't want to be like any of them. That was one of the great things about Prince. He had a lot of people imitating him, but he wasn't imitating anybody.

What was the first song recorded for this particular album?

Chronologically, it would have to be "Slow Love" and "I Could Never Take the Place of Your Man," because they were done years before the album was conceived. As I said before, the record wasn't done in any chronological order. As I recall, "Play in the Sunshine" was one of the last songs we did. When we sequenced the record, we needed a song to go between two of the really important songs. It was kind of like a palate cleanser. He would write a song just to put in the sequence, so that the sequence would make sense. That's why "Play in the Sunshine" was one of the last ones done. "I Could Never Take the Place of Your Man" and "Slow Love" were pulled out of the vault to be those segue songs, just to help finish this record and get it out there, so he didn't have to write another ballad. He said, "I don't feel like writing another ballad. I have an old song. Let's put "Slow Love" on there. Let's put it on there." "I Could Never Take the Place of Your Man" was a good, long jam that would get us to "The Cross." It was absolutely perfect for that. Technically speaking, those songs came first. But I know the gist of your question: of the more important songs, which one came first? One of the first songs was "Sign 'O' the Times." It set the tone and mood for this record.

Let's delve into the making of some of the songs from *Sign "O" the Times*.

"Sign 'O' the Times" was new for him in terms of tone. It was a little bit new in terms of sound too. He just received the Fairlight CMI, and he was really getting into it. He did the song at Sunset Sound in the control room. The Fairlight was set up right in there behind the console. He did one instrument at a time, like he normally did. I was blown away by the lyrics. It was something slightly new for him. It was a soulful, beautiful performance. It was an exceptional record. Many musicians cite this song as one of their favorites. It was a really impressive track.

On "Adore," Prince was really hurt that R&B and soul radio stations weren't playing him as much as they used to. When I was driving around Los Angeles in 1979 and 1980, I was listening to the R&B and soul stations KACE-FM and KJLH-FM, and they were playing a lot of Prince. This is where I first heard Prince after his first record came out. After *Purple Rain*, R&B radio had kind of given him up. They liked "Kiss" and some of his other stuff, but it wasn't the normal R&B and soul thing you would hear. He wanted that core audience back. He talked about that. "Adore" was an attempt to get more R&B radio play. It was an old-fashioned R&B and soul ballad. Lyrically, as well as the horn arrangements, the tempo, and everything about it, was R&B. I loved the high voice he put on the track. It was straight-up soul.

"The Ballad of Dorothy Parker" is an homage to the music he loved. He loved Kate Bush and Joni Mitchell. Prince had a strong feminine sensibility and those writers are sophisticated in a different way. He valued jazz chords and very poetic lyrics. Wendy and Lisa were fans of Joni Mitchell, but Prince was a huge fan. When he learned about the poet Dorothy Parker, he had a dream one night that was conflating Joni Mitchell and Dorothy Parker. It was a pretty vivid dream. He came running down to the studio, and he wanted to record it right away before it slipped out of his head. We just finished taking the delivery of this DeMedio console at his home on Galpin Boulevard, and we weren't done troubleshooting it yet. He said, "I don't care what condition it's in. If we can record with it, I just want to record *now*."

I replied, "Okay." And against my better judgement, we put on fresh tape, and we did that song from top to bottom. I spent the next twenty-four hours thinking, "What on earth did I do to this?" Because the song sounded like it was underwater. There was no high end. Prince just wouldn't stop. He kept on recording and recording and doing more overdubs. He didn't mind it because the song came to him in a dream. Maybe that's why he liked that underwater, muffled-sound quality to it. I remember when we were finally finished, I made him a cassette. He was getting ready to go upstairs to bed. He gave me some final instructions. Then he said, "I like the console, but it's kind of dull, isn't it?" [*laughs*] After he went to bed, I was able to pull out the voltmeter, and I saw that one of the two power supplies were down. It would be like a car running on half of its power. Once I fixed that problem, the console was great. It was another one of those happy accidents that he didn't mind at all.

Prince. Promotional photo for the concert film *Sign "O" the Times*.

Being that you were his right-hand person during this time, it was obvious that he trusted you with handling his overall sound. What was it like working alongside him while crafting this album?

I came to him as an audio technician to repair his equipment to keep it running. He expected that, after everything was hooked up and running properly, that I was going to be his engineer. I came to his camp without any engineering skills. I knew how to use the equipment, but I wasn't an engineer. An engineer is more of an artist. So he taught me his sound. I learned from him what he liked. I learned what EQ, reverbs, delays, and signal processing he liked. I became very adept at getting his sound for him. What were really the constant themes for me were gratitude, appreciation, and a strong determination to do everything humanly possible to facilitate his work. It mattered a great deal to me that I stayed up longer than him, because he would go to bed, and I'd be in the studio pulling patch cords, putting all the wires away, and making copies of things. I would routinely get fewer hours of sleep than he did, because I had to be the last one out and the first one back in the studio. I tried really, really hard to be what he needed. I wanted to serve this man that I admired and who I knew was a genius and did great work. My attitude back then was, "Just let me keep up. Don't make any mistakes. Just keep this train rolling." [*laughs*] It was a pleasure and a privilege to work with him. I recognized that we were doing great work and it was selling and he was popular. I was young just like he was, but I had no preconception of how history would view him. I thought he was great, but I came in thinking he was great. I knew we sold a whole lot of records and so did other people like Bruce Springsteen, Michael Jackson, Madonna, and other bands that were coming up, like U2, and became huge. So I had no way of knowing what would happen thirty or forty years later. All that mattered to me back then was to get these records made. ◉

At the end of 1987, Prince had a sudden revelation and decided to pull his impending visceral release, *The Black Album*, immediately going to work on its replacement, an artful record about love and sex titled LOVESEXY, whose subsequent tour saw Prince at the height of his performance powers.

CHANGE OF HEART

by Dan Dodds

"This is not music, this is a trip," Prince chanted, like a mantra, to the encore of "Alphabet St." At the close of 1987, stung by the relative commercial disappointment of his masterpiece, *Sign "O" the Times*—especially when compared to the triumphant, diamond-selling, Black-pop return of Michael Jackson's *Bad*—Prince believed he still had much to prove, particularly with his original Black American fan base, who he felt had deserted him, not just to his archrival, but also to, in his mind, the ultimate pretenders of funk: the emerging rap and hip-hop stylists. Canceling the *Black Album*—the notorious, knee-jerk reaction to his opponents—Prince instead embarked upon the more personal, idiosyncratic *Lovesexy* project; a platform for his most ambitious show to date and, arguably, his greatest work. A theatrical testimony of good conquering evil, it was a tour from which his band, his management, and indeed his art would never recover. It was a trip all right.

"Thing is, I don't believe in God, but when Prince asks you to sing 'God is love, love is God'—you do that; you don't question him," explains Dutch fan Rob Bemelen, who was there to witness Prince at the Westfalenhalle Stadium, in Dortmund, Germany, on September 9, 1988. It was a televised event, broadcast live to the whole of Europe. "That's the power he had over us," continues Rob, still in awe of the experience. "It was like a collective togetherness, for all eleven thousand of us."

The pivotal moment came at the end of the first act, when, having spent the previous hour wallowing in the filth of his most sinister classics—songs like "Sister," "Head," and "Jack U Off"—Prince struck up the solitary keyboard intro to the devotional epic "Anna Stesia." Essentially a Euro-soul hybrid in sound design; stark like Ultravox's "Vienna" before swirling into a rousing, twisted-gospel workout. Prince utilized the expertise at hand of his seasoned players who were primed coming off their concert film *Sign "O" the Times*—the all-star, rainbow-slop combo of she-funk heroine Sheila E.; bass player Levi Seacer Jr.; rhythm guitarist Miko Weaver; electric church powerhouse Boni Boyer; Madhouse sax player Eric Leeds; trumpet-musketeer Atlanta Bliss; triple threat Cat Glover (his greatest dancer, choreographer,

and rapper); and of course, ex-Revolution synth-stalwart Doctor Fink ("Doctorrr!"). While the band members all stand guard, Prince, seated at the piano in the center of the round, is lifted two stories high on a hydraulic platform, his arms outstretched in worship, bathed in a sunburst of spotlight. The song's impassioned performance matched its deeper meaning and significance, recounting the events of Tuesday, December 1, 1987, or "Blue Tuesday," as immortalized in the *Lovesexy '88* tour program.

Perhaps Blue Tuesday is the most speculated night in Prince-lore for two reasons: firstly, it was when Prince met Ingrid Chavez, aka Spirit Child; "A beautiful girl, the most" is how he described her, in a verse of "Anna Stesia" (long before Mayte Garcia, Prince's future wife, appropriated the title). Secondly, it was the infamous night when, inspired by an "epiphany," Prince felt compelled to cancel *The Black Album*.

"Do you believe?" he asked, as the band played out the vamp; the crowd roared "yes!" in response. Prince then abandoned the microphone and dropped his instrument, uncommonly exposed for a brief moment. "There's a new power in this house tonight," he says, off-mic to guitarist Miko Weaver, visibly moved. "Take this with you forever."

The Lovesexy band: (clockwise from top left) Cat Glover, Doctor Fink, Miko (kneeling), Eric Leeds, Levi Seacer Jr., Atlanta Bliss, Sheila E., Prince, and Boni Boyer. Photo by Jeff Katz for an album promotional poster.

Blue Tuesday

In Minneapolis, sometimes it snows in April. In winter, it's cold as hell.

On Tuesday, December 1, 1987, it was four below freezing outside. Poet Ingrid Chavez was in a bar called Williams Pub, waiting alone for a friend; thinking about braving the chill. "That's when Prince walked in," says Ingrid, gently, like rain is wet and sugar is sweet. "I had actually seen him before, at First Avenue, but I didn't know then if he noticed me. This time, I could tell he *was* watching me, and so I sat at the bar and sent him a cute note," Ingrid says, rolling her eyes and breaking into a chuckle. "Yeah, I know—classic."

The note read: "Hi, remember me? Probably not, but that's okay. Smile, I love it when you smile." Gilbert Davison, Prince's bodyguard, acted as the go-between. Prince was wearing little mirror-heart bracelets. He gave one to Ingrid, placed it on her wrist. "He asked me what my name was, and so I said, 'Gertrude,' and he said his name was 'Dexter,'" Ingrid laughs. "That's what we called each other." It was a week before the *The Black Album* was due to be released—not that Ingrid was aware of that, being more into the Cure and Ryuichi Sakamoto. "I wasn't really following him musically at the time," she admits. "I was totally out of context in his life; I was like this person that just dropped in."

Instead of going to his crib, which might have offered a more intimate setting, Dexter had Gilbert drive him and Gertrude forty-five minutes out of town to his new ten-million-dollar recording complex, Paisley Park. Upon arriving, Prince ushered Ingrid into a rehearsal room, which, she says, had been "pimped out in candles, drapes, and feathers." Leaving her alone to write, he then disappeared.

Alan Leeds—Prince's tour manager and the management rep on behalf of managers Bob Cavallo and Steven Fargnoli—recalls, "I was awakened by a call from our [Paisley Park] office manager, Karen Krattinger. Karen worked very closely as a personal assistant to Prince, and he had called her in the middle of the night insisting that *The Black Album* be stopped."

"I was actually there when he canceled the album," says Cat Glover, who remembers being seated with Prince at the kitchen table. "He opened up his heart and told me things that I'm sure he had never told anyone before. He loved that album, but it seemed dark to him. Something hit him that night that made him change—an enlightenment, a higher power."

The black dog of *The Black Album*, as a concept (though not necessarily the individual songs themselves, as Prince would include the gorgeous "When 2 R in Love" on *Lovesexy* and delight in performing selections on his next tour), appeared tethered to the negative feelings he was experiencing at the time, in both his life and his music. The desolate and as yet unreleased "Grand Progression"—recorded just weeks before *The Black Album* was compiled—perhaps offers the most meaningful insight into his mind-set at this point. Questioning his faith, Prince sings, "If there really is a God up above," sounding like he's four bars from cutting his ear off.

"He had shown signs of depression," says Alan. "On the personal side, I believe he was reaching the point where he longed for a meaningful romantic relationship in place of the rotating girlfriends he was known for. *The Black Album* was also made at a time when he was struggling to find direction. For the first time in his career, he was feeling threatened by young artists and peers, and more significantly, the rise and crossover of hip-hop into the mainstream. In a sense, he was wrestling with maintaining his place at the *cutting edge* of music."

"We all felt *The Black Album* would have been an interesting thing to happen for him," says saxophonist (and Alan's brother) Eric Leeds. "Prince was an artist who was very determined not to be pigeonholed as an R&B act, but there was a feeling that he had been losing support from his Black base." The competition was cranking up. Funk-lite, white-skinned British pop-start George Michael had unexpectedly conquered the *Billboard* R&B charts, an audience that hadn't been quite as effusive in support of *Sign "O" the Times* (and by association, the R&B masterwork "Housequake," a song many believe to be an unnoticed attempt to subjugate hip-hop). Michael Jackson's number one crossover hit *Bad* had also retained its core audience.

With Ingrid Chavez still waiting in the rehearsal room at Paisley Park, Prince summoned ex-employee, recording engineer Susan Rogers to a late-night rendezvous. It was Rogers, talking to Per Nilsen, the editor of Prince fanzine *Uptown*, who noticed that Prince's pupils seemed dilated. That it looked like he was tripping. According to Alan, "Everyone began speculating on what might have so dramatically changed Prince's mind about the record."

Artist: Prince
Album: *Lovesexy*
Label: Paisley Park
Release year: 1988
Performed, produced, and composed by: Prince
Engineered and mixed by: Joe Blaney, Eddie Miller, and Prince
Recorded at: Paisley Park
Drums, percussion, and vocal: Sheila E.
Computer keyboards: Doctor Fink
Vocal: Cat
Brass and vocals: Eric Leeds and Atlanta Bliss
Guitar and vocal: Miko
Vocal and Hammond organ: Boni Boyer
Bass and vocal: Levi Seacer Jr.
The Spirit Child on various songs is: Ingrid
Cover photo by: Jean Baptiste Mondino

Prince at Feijenoord Stadion in Rotterdam, Netherlands, during the August 17–19, 1988, shows of his historic *Lovesexy '88* tour.
Photo by FG/Bauer-Griffin/Getty Images.

"Sheila E. and I were in Los Angeles, doing *The Tonight Show* with my brother Alan that night," remembers Eric Leeds. "Early the next morning, at the airport, Alan said, all jaunty, 'Okay, got some news for you!'" laughs Eric, "and my first reaction was 'Oh shit!' I was very disappointed that it was shelved for a very practical reason—I owned a song on that album!" To lose out was the brilliant "Rock Hard in a Funky Place," including Eric's nasty sax line (plucked from an unreleased, jazzy Leeds original called "Pacemaker"). "As time went on, we started to hear all the different stories about what had really transpired that night," Eric adds. It was rumored that Prince—clean living and teetotal—had experimented with drugs.

"Yeah, he did do ecstasy that night," confirms Cat, matter-of-factly. "I was with him. Ecstasy is a drug that—they give it to couples who are having marital problems—it makes you feel loved, it makes you feel sexy." Despite the insinuation that Prince had suffered a "bad" trip on December 1, all of the accounts of what he actually said to people appear to suggest the opposite as being true: he was telling acquaintances how much he loved them, and that he felt he had experienced a spiritual awakening. So much so that in the new light of day, on December 2, Prince was still feeling the profound effect of what had happened the night before.

"It was romantic," says Ingrid, who, incredibly, was completely unaware until this interview that there were rumors that Prince was on something. "We fell in love with the poetry of who we were in each other's presence. We fell in love with words. I was not a great writer, but there was an innocence and rawness in what I wrote about that I think he felt he had lost. So when I think about the night we met, not knowing that he was high—though I can see it now—I think about the fact that the Ecstasy only acted as something that opened a door that he had held closed."

"She was the inspiration to Prince. He told me he had met this woman," Cat pauses, "and that her name was Gertrude."

Yes

When Warner Bros. chairman Mo Ostin personally sanctioned the cancellation, and withdrawal, of *The Black Album*, Prince immediately began work on its replacement, *Lovesexy*. Not concerned about playing it cool, Prince sent for Ingrid only days after their first meeting. The first track by Ingrid was a poem entitled "Cross the Line," recorded in the smaller Studio B. Spoken softly and sensuously, she recites: "In the distance, a light shines and someday he will touch it / Because it calls to him, says cross the line."

"I can still clearly remember Prince's face when he heard 'Cross the Line,'" says Ingrid. "He went quiet, and his eyes were really wide. I think there was something in that original recording that helped him make sense of the path he suddenly found himself on." Pleased with the initial results, Prince approved a full spoken-word project—with the working title *21 Poems*—and would hold back "Cross the Line" for a special assignment the following summer.

The first proper session for *Lovesexy* was recorded on December 11, 1987, in Studio A: a double-header consisting of an original composition, album closer "Positivity" and the *Crystal Ball* outtake "The Ball," reworked as the falsetto-led, jubilant album opener "Eye No."

As Alan told Per Nilsen about Prince, "His attitude changed, it was joyous music and he clearly enjoyed making it." Eric Leeds, who played saxophone on several *Lovesexy* tracks, recalls: "I did have an optimistic viewpoint in some of the sessions. Occasionally, I was able to hear some of the songs in their earliest versions and I was feeling, 'Okay, maybe this is going to be a little simpler, a little less produced perhaps?' But of course, that's not what happened. It was among the

first albums he'd done primarily at Paisley Park, and I think, being a forty-eight track studio, he seemed determined to use every track at his beck and call!"

Prince played the original version of the title track for Chairman Mo and Warner Bros. president Lenny Waronker out in Los Angeles, but they didn't get it, couldn't understand the lyrics. "We had put a horn chart on a song called 'Lovesexy,' which Prince took to L.A., and then a week or so later, Prince called us back to work on an entirely different song called, umm, 'Lovesexy,'" says Eric, who preferred the second/album version. (Incidentally, Cat believes the title *Lovesexy* itself is a play on the word ecstasy. As a hidden message, Prince did place the word "Ecstasy" within the "Alphabet St." video; he also put "Don't buy the *The Black Album*" in another frame, but it's interesting that he didn't attach any such instruction to the ecstasy hint.)

"Alphabet St.," recorded on New Year's Eve eve, 1987, is one of Prince's greatest-ever productions. It's him trying to out-funk the recent "Faith" in a "Roll-over George Michael" electronic rhythm and blues. Prince mixed the song while watching Cat dance, and also asked her to contribute vocals: "Cat, we need you to rap."

"He kept stopping me, saying, 'Nope,'" says Cat. "Shaking his head, 'Nope, nope. I don't like it. You have to do it again.' I started getting mad, so he said, 'Who's your favorite rapper? Salt-N-Pepa, right?'" Cat then adopts Prince's jokey, pimp-like, Cloreen Bacon Skin voice: "'Salt-N-Pepa ain't gon' like dis—you better rap like you mean it!'"

Ingrid features on "Alphabet St." too, reciting the alphabet. "Everybody says to me, 'What happened to G?!'" says Ingrid, laughing about the letter she missed. "He was trying to get me to steam it up, and well, I guess I got distracted."

It was a beautiful winter for Ingrid, creative and spiritually uplifting. "It was like being in a bunker for three months. Sometimes, you'd come out for air and then you'd go back in." Prince would take her to dinner, go clubbing, they'd go to the movies, play pool, and sometimes Prince's dad, John L. Nelson, would accompany them. But Ingrid never really mixed with the band, as she sort of felt like Yoko Ono. Says Ingrid: "Nobody wanted me there. There was a bunch of [bitchy] stuff going on, and I just didn't want to have anything to do with it. He never put me in that world, never exposed me to it." After completing the album, Ingrid didn't spend as much time with Prince, who turned his attention to the tour—*Lovesexy '88*. Several of Prince's staff still had misgivings about the new album, doubted its commercial appeal. "I remember Prince making a big deal about the record being played as a whole, in a complete suite, rather than sequenced into individual tracks," says Alan Leeds. "Something I felt obligated to point out would be a problem at radio, but he didn't care."

This Is Not Music—This Is a Trip

Production designer Roy Bennett had been with Prince since *Dirty Mind*. "He was really the unsung hero of the Prince tours, because Prince trusted him," says Eric. "Prince would go to Roy with abstract ideas about how he would like the show to look and Roy would flesh them out." A year or so before preparations started on *Lovesexy '88*, Roy had the opportunity to design Queen's Magic Tour—which turned out to be Freddie Mercury's last Queen tour before he died. Contractually, Prince had "first right of refusal," says Roy, who would have to clear it with management. They said, "Okay, Prince is busy in the studio, so that's fine."

Recalls Roy: "A week later, I get a call from Prince's managers, Bob Cavallo and Steve Fargnoli, and they're like, 'Can you fly to L.A.? We need to talk to you.' So I get there and sit in Bob's office and he goes, 'Prince has decided that he wants to do something and that you

(*top*) The *Lovesexy '88* tour program. Cover photo by Jeff Katz.
(*right*) Ticket to the *Lovesexy '88* filming at Westfalenhalle Stadium on September 9, 1988, at Dortmund, Germany. Courtesy of Rob Bemelen.

have to back out of the Queen thing.' And I said, 'That's really unfair!' And we're going back and forth, when all of sudden, the door opens and Prince walks in, where he must have been outside listening—'So you wanna work with Queen, huh?' And he said, 'What's the name of their single? "Princes of the Universe"?!' And he just started laughing, turned around, walked out, and slammed the door."

Prince intended to take the *Sign "O" the Times* show to the next level; wanted the *Lovesexy '88* stage to look like a playground for grown-ups, to be set in the round for stadiums, with a basketball hoop, a swing, a bed, a replica Ford Thunderbird car, a bridge, trellises and flowers, strobe lights and LED Plexiglas with multi-colored letters, with the entire production setting him back an alleged two million dollars. He also wanted a sailboat (for "I Wish U Heaven"), a waterfall, and a fountain; but after they couldn't get the fountain to work in the Paisley Park car park—water was pissing out everywhere, not good for such an electronically powered production—it was decided to stick with what they had.

Rehearsals were tedious, each song taking as long as ten hours to set up, with over forty song arrangements to be learned just in case Prince wanted to alter the track list.

"We'd be on the first song and then, after thirty seconds of it, Prince would yell, 'Stop!'" explains Eric, adding, "Then he and Roy would sit there for fifteen to thirty minutes, discussing the movements, lights, and all the effects. Then we'd do another minute and Prince would yell again, 'Everybody stop!'—this was the process. I tell you, I was so done with that show before we had even played the first gig!"

Rehearsals took around four months. Other band members were showing signs of fatigue. Boni Boyer was arguably the greatest vocalist to ever work in a Prince band. Raphael Saadiq grew up with Boni (who, sadly, passed away in 1996) and had played in her band back in the Bay Area. "Boni Boyer was like the Queen of Oakland," says Saadiq, "whether it was funk, house, or whatever."

"Boni and I were really close," says Cat Glover. "Duane [Nelson, Prince's brother,] used to say, 'What, are you guys like Wendy and Lisa now?'" Boni was not shy of telling Prince what she thought; used to give him lip. "We were doing a sound check," recalls Cat, "and Boni came in wearing silk pajamas. She looked really cute in a silk two-piece, but Prince made a joke. Using that voice he does, he said, 'You don't come on my stayyge wearin' no silk pajamas!' And Boni said, 'You got a nerve, you on this stage with a green jumpsuit wi' alphabets all over it!'" Everyone cracked up laughing.

Hundalasiliah!

"Clap your hands, stomp your feet—everybody," said Spirit Child, introducing the TV broadcast from Westfalenhalle Stadium, the thirty-first night of the world tour. The crowd, made up of predominantly Dutch fans, duly obliged. "They were massive fans of Prince, and were the best crowd ever," says Roy, "so we bussed a ton of them in from Holland to create the vibe for the live recording." Dutchman Rob Bemelen, who had already seen Prince twice that summer, had all the LPs: Madhouse, Sheila E.'s albums ("A Love Bizarre" had been a number seven hit in the Netherlands), and even owned an actual copy, not a bootleg, of *The Black Album*. "Yes, of course," states Rob, "I can't remember the name of the shop, it was in Nijmegen [Netherlands], a record store, or—*wrecka stow*." Rob laughs at his own fortune/ingenuity in referencing the film *Under the Cherry Moon*. His countrymen and women also knew all of the music, and were with Prince from the get-go as he rode into the arena, with Cat and Sheila E., on the Ford Thunderbird. "Snare drum pounds on the two and four," hollers Prince. "All the party people get on the floor—*bass!*" The band launches

into "Erotic City," the first song of Act 1: "The Dark," the section of the show almost entirely dedicated to the sleazier, more lustful, sexually themed work in Prince's canon. Sequenced like a long suite into a rich tapestry, incorporating old standards with new contemporary material, the songs fit like a *Lovesexy vs. the Black Album* super project—a story of good overcoming evil. "No one had ever attempted a theatrical show like that, an arena show in the round," says Roy Bennett. Prince strode onto the stage wearing a white suit with polka dots, his long black hair tied back behind his head, large hooped earring on his right ear—every step, every movement, every facial gesture, every flick of the hair carefully choreographed in an elaborate dance. "Prince was inspired by a guy named Moses Pendleton; he gave me a [video] cassette and told me to go to the hotel and watch it," explains Cat. "Moses was a dancer that worked in the theater who had a different way of doing everything. When he got out of bed in the morning, he made it a dance. He was awesome."

The potential for pretension tempered by the humor on display, like when Prince shushes the crowd as Cat sings to his crotch during "Head," then implores the audience to sing along to his most salacious lines, leading them astray. "I know you're nasty—say it."

The two additions from *The Black Album* are performed in their entirety. The dark 'n' freaky, S&M-themed "Superfunkycalifragisexy" is a debauched precursor to the funny, caustic, showstopper "Bob George," with Prince dressed in flamboyant shades and an alligator coat that, according to Cat, George Clinton gave to him. The song itself allegedly named after manager Bob Cavallo and music critic Nelson George. "I flew out for a *Purple Rain* gig and was disappointed that he seemed like he was trying very hard to replicate the movie onstage, and I wrote that in *Billboard*," explains Nelson George, adding, "I believe that's the genesis of 'Bob George.' I went and saw the *Purple Rain* show later in D.C., and I know he was aware I was in the building. He started that show in total darkness, jamming for several minutes, before doing a stellar show that had the fresh feeling of his earlier tours. I always thought the D.C. show was a bit of a 'fuck you' to me. But then I thought, 'I'm giving myself too much credit.' Then, years later, 'Bob George' comes out, so I definitely pissed him off at some point."

As the end of Act 1 nears, Prince—the old Prince—symbolically dies onstage as Eric Leeds, Atlanta Bliss, Miko Weaver, and Levi Seacer Jr. point their musical instruments at him and shoot. Then the emotional rendition of "Anna Stesia" signals his rebirth, bringing Act 1 to a close. Meanwhile, under the stage, Cat is getting ready for the next number. "I had to wear outfits under my outfits, which really wasn't a lot of clothes, as it was just underwear mainly," Cat laughs. "That wasn't my choice, but I'd be under the stage taking down a pair of thigh-high stockings and adding on another pair right above them, jumping straight back onstage. It was just energy."

For the "Intermission," Prince produced a specially made track, splicing an excerpt of a Jill Jones recitation from *Romeo and Juliet*. "Wow, flashback," says Jill. "We did that originally for 'Modernaire'; we had a whole [Shakespeare] soliloquy!" "Intermission" also used the aforementioned "Cross the Line" by Ingrid Chavez, adding samples of stunning Clare Fischer string arrangements from the vault. "In the distance, a light shines…," recited Ingrid over the sound system, while Cat danced a ballet.

"'I Wish U Heaven' was like a nightly relief," admits Alan Leeds, "a moment when we could all exhale, partly because the bulk of the show was behind us, and particularly because the lyrics were so inspiring. My wife, Gwen, was my assistant on the tour. She and a couple of the wardrobe staff might only watch that one song and often returned to the production office with tears of joy in their eyes."

Prince (background), Sheila E., and Cat during a *Lovesexy '88* concert on July 28, 1988, in London, England. Photo by FG/Bauer-Griffin/Getty Images.

Sheila E. was big in Holland in her own right, and the audience would chant "Sheila E.! Sheila E.! Sheila E.!" So Prince would let her know that it was his stage by performing the duet "A Love Bizarre" on his own.

"He would go, 'You gotta sing "I Wish U Heaven" [his new single], and Sheila would go, 'Which one? Was that a hit?' " remembers Cat. "We'd be like, 'Uh-oh, here they go again!' " At the end of "Glam Slam," after another punishing routine, Prince gave Cat a handshake. "He said, 'Good job. You tore it up tonight,' " says Cat.

The piano break was a highlight of the show: Prince took to the stage solo, dressed in a black eighteenth-century gentleman's frock coat with a cane, like an uptown Amadeus Mozart. Just Prince, a microphone, and a grand piano. A recital of beautiful renditions of "When 2 R in Love," the instrumental "Venus de Milo," and the audience-assisted "Condition of the Heart." He also righted the wrongs of the concert-film version of *Sign "O" the Times* by playing songs that weren't included in the film like the adult nursery rhyme "Starfish and Coffee" and "Strange Relationship"—at his most charismatic and relaxed, shamelessly showing off his virtuosity. At one point, he teases the crowd for being too mawkish and singing "I think I love her" on "Raspberry Beret." Michael Jackson was never this good, and Mozart couldn't dance.

Integrated into "The Light" act of the *Lovesexy* set, the encore/hits are elevated to musical nirvana. The hit "1999" finds a natural setting, as the mother of all concert finales, "I got a lion in my pocket, y'all," Prince sings. "Her name is Boni B."

Still on high from becoming soccer champions of Europe earlier that summer of '88, the Netherlands beating West Germany on their own patch, the crowd sings, "Olé, Olé, Olé, Olé!" essentially taking over Dortmund: a reverse invasion, lapping up every riff, the sax line from Madhouse's "Three," and singing along, en masse, to a concise—truly stunning—four-minute version of "Purple Rain." With Prince's spirituality reborn, he forsakes his "let me guide you" messiah-like aspirations by dedicating the song, wholeheartedly, "One time for the man above."

"That was the one, of all the shows I've seen," says Rob Bemelen in astonishment. "The way he played the guitar. That was the one."

The Aftershow

The *Lovesexy* tour aftershows were legendary. "Me and my friend Raymond van Oosterhout tried to go. We had gone to the previous Rotterdam [Netherlands] shows, but for the third show, on the nineteenth [of August], we didn't have a ticket," explains Rob. "We thought, 'What if we just get a car, go to Rotterdam, and see what happens?' So we waited outside the stadium, and when it was done, a black Mercedes with blacked-out windows left with high speed. Our Subaru Justy, one of those little Japanese cars, kept up for about two or three miles, but when he got onto the highway, he was gone!"

Eric Leeds missed the aftershow with the most infamy—because of its heavily bootlegged status—at the Paard van Troje, in the Hague, Netherlands. "Everybody asks me, 'So, where was the saxophone that night?' And I say, 'I'm afraid the saxophone was in bed asleep.' " Eric pulled a sickie because Prince unnecessarily arranged a photo shoot earlier that day. "If he was bugged about something then the rest of us had to be bugged about it too!" Eric laughs. Prince made his point though—gave everyone a bonus that showed up that night, except Eric. "It was money well spent from my perspective." Prince was in a bad mood that night, as captured by the bootleg. When performing the stripped-back, Rhodes-laced "Still Would Stand All Time," he can be heard reprimanding Boni Boyer for getting a lyric wrong. "Who's the

(top) Sheila E., Prince, and and Cat at Feijenoord Stadion before the show. Photo by FG/Bauer-Griffin/Getty Images.
(above) Prince and his band at Feijenoord Stadion in 1988 in Rotterdam, Netherlands. (left to right) Doctor Fink, Eric Leeds, Cat, Miko (in back), Prince, Boni Boyer, Sheila E., Atlanta Bliss, and Levi Seacer Jr. Photo by FG/Bauer-Griffin/Getty Images.

fool singing 'Will'? It's '*Would*'!"

"Yeah, Boni flipped him the bird one night!" remembers Roy Bennett, who laughs. "It was like, no matter how good they were, it was never good enough, and he had no qualms about calling you out in front of the audience if you screwed up, in front of everybody."

Back home in the U.S., tensions were mounting. Ticket sales had not been great and the tour was losing money, especially since the show was in the round and there were hundreds of obstructed-view seats that couldn't be sold. "During the course of the tour, Prince's relationship with managers Steve Fargnoli and Bob Cavallo had seriously soured," Alan notes. "He tended to blame them for every empty venue seat, as well as the less than spectacular reception given the album and its singles. I became a ping-pong ball between them." (Prince even tried to withdraw the second single, "Glam Slam," at the last minute; but this time, Warner Bros. weren't having any of it.)

Prince and his management stopped speaking, and eventually Fargnoli and Cavallo were replaced. "We all appreciated that the show was brilliantly creative and technically innovative," says Alan. "But it was our first real U.S. tour since *Purple Rain*. Whereas on that tour, we might sell out a major-city arena for four or five nights, on *Lovesexy*, we barely sold out one or two nights." On returning to Chanhassen, Minnesota, Alan became vice president of Paisley Park Records. *Lovesexy '88* would be his last tour with Prince.

Most of the band had reached burnout with Prince and left after *Lovesexy '88*. Only Miko, Levi, and Doctor Fink stayed on. While Cat remained close with Prince (he worked on her unreleased Warner Bros. project, *I Am Energy*), she left with Steve Fargnoli after refusing Prince's request to fire him. Ingrid Chavez reconnected with Prince and would go on to star in *Graffiti Bridge*, his next movie project, with her debut album, *May 19th, 1992*, released on Paisley Park Records

(following Madonna's platinum-selling "Justify My Love," a song cowritten by Lenny Kravitz and Chavez, who went uncredited until she sued Kravitz).

"I had an apartment in Minneapolis city center above a barbershop on Lyndale and Twenty-fifth—*or something*," Ingrid says, straining to remember. There was a jazz bar below, and I saw Prince go in. So I went down, spoke to Duane Nelson outside, and gave him a six-song cassette of some new music. About a week later, I came home and I couldn't get in my apartment—it was filled with flowers, addressed to 'Gertrude.'"

Cash-strapped and having to take on the soundtrack to Tim Burton's *Batman* movie, Prince would never again hit the peak of the *Lovesexy '88* show, his greatest achievement, nor would he make art as brilliant as "Alphabet St." or "Anna Stesia." The *Lovesexy '88* live broadcast would be released on VHS, but in a commercially motivated switch would have Act 2, "The Light," released first as *Livesexy 1* followed by Act 1, "The Dark," as *Livesexy 2*; denying those fans unable to attend of the sheer brilliance of the original concept.

"I remember telling my parents, 'Please set the VCR at nine, the show starts at nine!'" says Rob, adding, "So I went to Dortmund, by bus, by coach, and when I got back, it was the middle of the night, around 2:00 AM, but I couldn't sleep. So I went into the living room, put on the TV, my headphones, and I watched the entire show again." ◉

After a few commercially questionable releases, Prince set out to generate hits and regain his R&B audience with DIAMONDS AND PEARLS, which featured new backup band the New Power Generation and elements of hip-hop. Guitarist and bandleader Levi Seacer Jr. and engineer Michael Koppelman share their recollections of the recording of the 1991 album.

NEW BIRTH

by Chris Williams

How did you begin working with Prince?

Levi Seacer Jr.: It's kind of complicated. I'll try to do a little condensed version. I was with Sheila Escovedo [stage name Sheila E.]. We used to play jazz and funk music in the Bay Area. About a year after that, Sheila left the Bay Area. She went on tour with Marvin Gaye. Then she hooked up with Prince, and they worked on [her album] *In the Glamorous Life*. Sheila did her thing. Now during that time, Prince had a group called the Family. So he was looking for a guitarist for that band. Sheila said to him, "Oh, I know somebody in the Bay Area." They flew me out to Minneapolis, but I didn't meet Prince at first. I was just in that circle. I auditioned for the Family's band and actually got the gig. I had the gig for two days, and then something came up and Prince sent a message saying, "Oh, man. I really liked you, but I had to do some other things with that. Man, you're hot. It's cool. I'm going to keep you in mind." Anyway, Prince came to San Francisco to visit, because he was up here a lot because of Sheila E. He was very hands-on with all the bands. Sheila was his protégé act. He would come to San Francisco to check her out randomly. So this time when he came, I was in her band on bass. He said, "Hey, didn't you just audition for the Family on guitar?" I replied, "Yeah, but I play a little bass too. I play a couple of instruments like you." He laughed. That was my first time really getting to meet him, so I was in the camp. Now, how did I get in Prince's band? After Prince disbanded the Revolution, this was about two years into my career with Sheila, he decided to put a new band together. It wasn't officially called the New Power Generation at the time. He took Sheila, Boni [Boyer], and me, and he rounded it out with some other players. We all worked from Minneapolis to form the first version of the New Power Generation. So that's how I got into Prince's band.

Were you there when he started adding members to New Power Generation, and were you involved with selecting the other musicians?

Levi Seacer Jr.: The first band had me, Sheila, Boni, and Miko [Weaver]. Miko used to be in Sheila's band, but Prince took Miko from Sheila's band and put him into the Family. The reason I was auditioning for the Family was because he was going to replace Miko with me. But they worked things out. Then, Prince put Miko back into the first version of the New Power Generation. Basically, the rhythm section was all from the Bay Area. So you had me on bass, Sheila on drums, Boni Boyer was on keys and vocals, and Miko was on rhythm guitar. Then he had Eric Leeds [on saxophone] who was already in Minneapolis. He kept Atlanta Bliss on trumpet and then Doctor Fink [on keys] and Cat [Glover on backup vocals and dance]. If you remember *Sign "O" the Times*, that was our first project. But we still weren't officially called the New Power Generation yet.

***Diamonds and Pearls* was the first album where your band was featured as the New Power Generation. The influence of hip-hop was prevalent on this album. What was Prince's approach as you saw it?**

Levi Seacer Jr.: Prince never thought of himself as a commercial artist. But when we did *Diamonds and Pearls*, I think, if you were to look in his diary, he would say, "Okay, *Diamonds and Pearls* was supposed to be sort of a commercial R&B-pop album but with the Prince influence." In other words, we were going for some hits. We were kind of going straight down the middle of the road, but the way we'd like to do it. I don't think Prince would have said it like that back then, but it's in hindsight. It was kind of like when he did *The Black Album*. The reason he did that album was because people said, "Prince ain't funky no more." I was there. He said, "What? Do you speak English?" He took like three weeks and made the hardest funk he could think of and that was *The Black Album*. It was a similar kind of thing. People were saying, "Damn. We like the *Lovesexy* work, and we think it's real creative, but I don't know, can Prince make the hits again?" That kind of thing. And he was very competitive. He was like, "I know how to do that all day long; that's easy." [*laughs*]

During that time, going from *Sign "O" the Times* to *The Black Album*, and then to *Lovesexy*, the *Batman* soundtrack, and *Graffiti Bridge*, as you were saying, people were questioning whether or not he could still come up with the goods. What was his mind-set going into the making of this album when people were questioning him?

Levi Seacer Jr.: Well, even though he didn't really care about the commercial stuff like that, he always felt like a real true artist would do what they did. There would be times when things hit and times when they didn't. But in the long run, if an artist made a good record, people were going to come back and say, "You know what, I need to go back and listen to that again, because that was some good music," I would say on *Diamonds and Pearls*, he was like, "I need to show them that I can do what they're doing, but I can do it better than them. [*laughs*] I'm going to do cool commercial and cool, you know what I mean?" He was like, "I need to show y'all something, just in case y'all forgot." [*laughs*] I liked that about him. You know, he could do whatever he wanted. He was like, "I can make hits, and I can make creative stuff." That was his mind-set. I think, if he were to open his diary and talk like I'm talking to you, he would have said it like that.

When he was working on the material for this record, did he demo any of his songs before bringing them to you guys? Or was it kind of like a process where a lot of this stuff evolved from jam sessions?

Levi Seacer Jr.: No, he didn't do any demos. A typical recording session for us would be just bringing a notepad, and he may have had tons of notes and stuff. For example, songs like "Push" and "Willing and Able" were just ideas. And he was like, "Hey, let's fool around with something. I'm kind of hearing the beat like this." He would allow us to kind of take that seed of an idea and turn it into a song. There were occasions where he was in the studio recording a song, and then he would bring us in to give it kind of a band sound. For four of those basic tracks, we did them all in one day. We were in Japan, and we had a little time off. One day, I was practicing, just kind of grooving on bass, and he said, "Hey, what's that?" I said, "Oh, just something I was messing around with." He said, "Michael, put a beat to that." Michael put a beat to it, and then he had some notes. He was working on a song titled "Willing and Able," but he didn't have any music for it yet. He was like, "This will work fine for that." So that's how that came together. For "Diamonds and Pearls," he had that one written. He wanted to actually start a cut on that one. He was about fifty percent done when he brought us in, and we put our last colors on it.

Can you describe what the band's rehearsal sessions were like?

Levi Seacer Jr.: People always ask me, "Hey, did you have fun?" I quickly say, "No"—and put a *p* on it: "*Nope*." I put a *p* on it, okay? They're like, "Oh, come on, man," No, no, no, it wasn't fun. There was

no fun. That wasn't the point of it. I always share this story, and I'll share it with you. I remember the first night of the *Sign "O" the Times* tour, and that was my first tour night with him. Just before the show began, the band was looking a little worn out because we had worked so hard. Prince looked at us and said, "What's wrong with y'all? You're tired?" He said, "Guess what? I don't care, I don't really care. The show is for the people who have paid and for the fans. They've been saving up their money to come see us. I don't really care if you have a good time. As a matter of fact, that'll keep you more alert." [*laughs*] "We're here to play to the peak of our perfection for people who love our music. So you all got that. Now, if you have a day when you have a good time, then that's wonderful, but I'm not here to make sure that you have a good time playing with Prince. Is that clear?" [*laughs*] I remember, about a week into the tour, I said to him, "Good luck tonight." He said, "Don't say that," and I was like, "Okay, what did I say wrong?" He was like, "It's not about luck. We are good because we practice. Don't call it luck. I'm going to have a good show because I practiced. Even on my worst night, the show is still going to be good because we've practiced. We're a well-oiled machine." That was the genius of Prince.

This is what Prince used to do. So, if we had a three-month tour, we would rehearse for three months. If it was a six-month tour, we would rehearse for five or six months. Most people get together for two weeks and then go on tour. No, we rehearsed for the same length as the tour. We were doing six days a week, ten to twelve hours a day, and that was just for rehearsal. That wasn't including recording sessions at night, or playing at clubs on the weekend. That was our schedule. I remember the first day in his band. We were all there and he said, "Okay, everybody listen up. This is how I want stuff. Rehearsal is not for rehearsal." I had to let that sink in for a minute, and I was like, "What does he mean by that?" He said, "Listen, we don't come to rehearsal learning the songs." This was during the *Sign "O" the Times* album. He said, "Listen, I'm going to give you three songs a night. Okay, so if you play bass, you need to learn the bass part and the vocals part. If you play the keys, you need to learn the keys and vocal parts. You need to learn the song at home, okay. And on the following day, I'm going to count the song off, and it better sound like a record." [*laughs*] So he said, "Rehearsal is for me to dissect the songs and decide what the arrangements will be—I might want to take a verse out, or I might want to give this a try, but I can't do that if y'all don't know the songs well, so you learn the songs in their entirety and then I'll do the tracking when we get to rehearsal. Don't come to rehearsal learning stuff." A few people tried to test him a little bit, and that didn't work out too well for them. He made a big deal about that, and a couple people got fired. So we learned twenty-one songs in seven days. And we're talking about Prince songs that had serious arrangements. It was intense in that way. Now, if you did your homework and came there prepared, you would be all right. But if you came not knowing your stuff, it was going to be a bad day. A real bad day.

When you moved like that, you could accomplish so much. You could've came to see Prince for ten days straight, and every day would be different, because he had the band at that kind of level. We were always used to changing stuff. As a matter of fact, after the three months of rehearsing for a three-month tour, the first day of the tour we changed almost the whole show. Prince would be like, "Okay, you all did a good job, but now we're performing in front of people. Now, I got these notes. On song one, take out the bridge, and on song number three, I wrote a whole new part for it." He gave us two hours of note changes, and we got to make the changes then and played them that night. Mind you, we were videotaping and recording every night, and he was listening to everything every night. It was very intense.

(*opposite*) Levi Seacer Jr. during Prince's ACT II tour in Gent, Belgium, 1993. Photo by Gie Knaeps/Getty Images.

Let's transition to your band and Prince's studio routine during the making of this album. Was there a set time that you guys would go into the studio to work on material, or was it just pretty much whenever Prince felt like going into the studio?

Levi Seacer Jr.: I spent a lot of time with Prince when I was with Sheila. Prince did a lot of recording at Sunset Sound [in Los Angeles]. When I joined Sheila's band, he would invite me to his sessions to play. I was sitting there with Wendy and Lisa, and I wasn't in his band, but we all jammed together for years. When I got in his band, he remembered that I liked doing studio stuff, and he said, "You got some studio chops. You like to write a bit. Levi, I am going to tell you this once. Are you listening?" And I said, "Yes, man. I am listening." He said, "Listen, we do ten to twelve hours of rehearsal." Some people started at nighttime, but we weren't like that. We would start at ten in the morning. After ten hours, he'd say, "Okay, Levi. I'm in the studio. I'm going to say this once. If you want to work with me in the studio, I just gave you my schedule. So if you show up, then I know you're serious. If you don't, then okay. I'm just going to say he does the band thing. He's not that interested in the studio thing." But I took him up on it. So he'd have his dinner, and sure enough, like clockwork, every night, an hour after rehearsal, he was in there recording something. I'd be sitting right there, he'd say, "Oh, you showed up!"

Now, as far as how long his sessions would go, I am not going to lie, we pulled some all-nighters. We'd be coming out of there at six in the morning, and then be back at rehearsal at ten in the morning. When he would do it, and I actually liked doing it this way, Prince wouldn't leave the studio until the song was at least seventy percent formed. If we started off with nothing, by the time we left the studio, we might have recorded two or three songs in one night. They were all going to be at seventy percent level. In other words, they would be almost ready to mix. It was just as intense as rehearsal. He used to laugh and say, "Listen. I know you're tired from the studio, but I'm expecting everything in rehearsal tomorrow, okay. They are two separate things. You got that?" I said, "Yeah, I got it, man, I got it." Every now and then, we might get out of there at midnight, but it was usually at four or five in the morning and that was for six days a week, too. I mean, he was just music, music, music, which explains why there are so many songs in his vault. Prince was doing two or three songs, at seventy percent level six days a week, for his whole career. So you're talking about thousands of songs, not in this ideal form but recorded with vocals, production, everything. It's mind-boggling. When they talk about the vault, it's like the world doesn't have a clue. I heard a lot of stuff from the vault, man. It's some stuff in there, man. You'll be like, "How could he not have put this out?" [laughs]

One day, Prince said to me, "Levi, I want you to hear something. You remember when you heard 'When Doves Cry'?" I said, "Prince, I have to be honest with you, man. When you put that out, I thought you made one of the biggest mistakes." When "When Doves Cry" came out, it was nothing but drums and vocals. I was like, "Where's all the production?" But after a while, it caught on. I thought it was kind of cool. He said, "Okay. Now check this out." He sat me down, and he played me the original version of "When Doves Cry." Man, there were one hundred violins on it, guitars, basses, and all this other stuff. I said, "Man, okay, okay. How could you record all that and decide to break it down to vocals and drums? That was a big decision." He said, "Yeah, man. I just wanted to do something really different, and I wanted people to get used to a different kind of sound. I knew it was drastic, but I took a gamble on it and, you know, it paid off." I said, "Yeah, it came out, but oh my God." What I'm trying to tell you is, when the world actually hears the real version of "When Doves Cry,"

they're going to freak out, man. [laughs] There was this beautiful, lush orchestra on there. It's crazy. [laughs]

That's just one of thousands of songs. I brought that up to say that a lot of the songs in the vault were precursors to the final production like "Gett Off." There were ten versions of that before he got to the final one. I was there to watch the whole thing. The song is still "Gett Off," but he redid it about ten times to get to that final one that you heard. He said, "Man, something still ain't right." And all the other versions were cool. [laughs] I was like, "Man, to me, you were done on version four." He was like "No, no, no." When we used to work in the studio, I used to look in his eyes and you could tell when it was done and when it wasn't. When it wasn't, he would look up in the sky. It was almost like he was talking to a spirit, "It ain't there, we have to keep going." And until he actually took his eyes from the sky and looked straight across, that's when I knew it was done. Then it was time to mix that. It was hard, man, because the ideas he was doing getting up to the final ones were cool, but all of that kind of stuff went in the vault. I don't know of any artist on the planet who even has that kind of body of work. Because they'd have to write it, sing it, and play it. He did a lot of his own recording, too, like an engineer. They'd have to be able to do all of those things to even have a third of that kind of catalog. It's crazy, man. Then, they'd have to be prolific on top of that. You know what I mean? It's one thing to be like, "I worked really, really hard." But you could be working hard on some stuff that ain't happening. Here was a guy who could deliver, and he had a work ethic like that. That was rare.

It was definitely rare. When you guys were all in the studio, where was Prince positioned? Where were you positioned? Where were the other musicians positioned during studio sessions?

Levi Seacer Jr.: I basically put songs in two categories: it was either piano songs or guitar songs. If it was a song like "The Question of U" or "Diamond and Pearls," they started off as piano songs. Now, if we were doing some rock stuff that had guitar leads, then he would be on the guitar. Position-wise, the drummer was always in an isolated room with glass. Prince would always be facing us when we recorded. On *Diamonds and Pearls*, I was on bass, so I'd usually be on the left of him. The keyboards would be slightly behind that and the drummer would be in the booth. We didn't do all of the vocals and the music at the same time. Sometimes, Prince would just have his stage mic there, and he would just throw down a scratch track, just so we knew the structure of a song, but then he would erase that and do it over later, after we built up the music. That was basically the configuration. There were a few times when we recorded everything at once. At Paisley Park, we had three isolation rooms, so you could put the horn section in one, the drums in another, and the vocalist in another. It was pretty isolated. It was usually lead guitar, rhythm, bass, keys and drums. That was the usual tracking system. Then, depending if it was a piano or guitar song, he would be on the piano or the guitar.

Can you talk about the collaboration between the band members during the making of this record?

Levi Seacer Jr.: Well, obviously, there were a few tunes on there with the rap stuff, so he and Tony Mosley were handling that kind of stuff. Now, I'll go on the record for this, because a lot of times the critics were brutal in their criticism of Tony. What the critics didn't know is even if Prince would've had a real super dope rapper or whatever, whoever was hot at the time, Prince would not have let them done

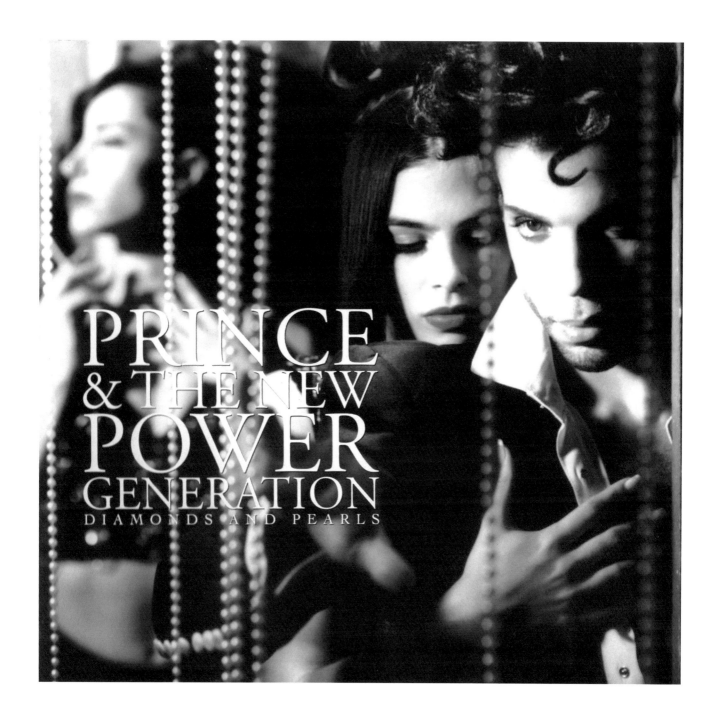

Artist: Prince and the New Power Generation
Album: *Diamonds and Pearls*
Label: Paisley Park
Release year: 1991
Performed, arranged, produced, and composed by: Prince and the New Power Generation
Engineered by: Michael Koppelman and Matt Larson
Recorded at: Paisley Park, Olympic Studios (London), Warner Pioneer Studios (Japan), and Larrabee Sound Studios (Los Angeles)
Cover photo by: Randee St. Nicholas

what they normally did, because Prince wasn't interested in just rap the way rap was. Prince was like, "I'm going to explore some different topics, and I need to add the musicality to it as well." So, in most rap music, it was beat driven and then you'd put your rhyme over that. So you were only dealing with two elements. But when you were dealing with a band, it was different. Prince always felt like you couldn't just come with your standard flow, because this was a musical band. We were playing the harps and the strings and things that come in, and also you couldn't just pick a subject that didn't fit with the music. In other words, to make a long story short, Tony wasn't allowed to write something that could've been competitive with other rappers. His challenge with Tony was like, "Man, yeah, I know. Don't listen to them, man, because we're trying to write stuff that will last for an eternity." Prince would be like, "We're trying to write music for the history of music not just a time period." Because even the great artists of the world, they didn't even like their paintings until they died. Prince was on that Picasso type of thing. "They ain't going to get it right now. But let's wait—let's go to the peak of what we can be, and then let time catch up with our work."

When I was with Sheila, we played a lot of jazz, jazz fusion, funk jazz, and funk soul. When I came to Prince, I felt like I brought that kind of thing into it. The musical arrangements got a little bit more intricate, and that was due to my background with Sheila. Sheila was in a band too. We would play Santana, George Duke, and all that kind of stuff. Prince always wanted to push the boundaries, because he was always learning as a musician too. But at that time, going from the Revolution sound to the New Power Generation sound was a change for him; Sheila, me, and the rest of the band kind of brought those elements. He said, "Okay, you guys can go there, and I've been wanting to go there, so let's go." I did a little bit of writing and producing on the album. I was his musical director, so some of the pieces that I would put into the live show, he ended up incorporating them into the album. Like on "Daddy Pop," there was a two-minute section on the song where the band jams. I added that in conjunction with the band during rehearsal, while Prince was out of town. He came back, and he put it in the show. When we were working on the album, he said, "You know that little piece y'all added on? I need y'all to add that on the song." We went back into the studio and recorded it and added it to "Daddy Pop." He was cool with us like that. It was the Prince show, but if he liked something, he would incorporate it into what he was doing. He was cool like that.

Talk to me about the synergy that the rest of the musicians—keyboardist Tommy Barbarella, bassist Sonny Thompson, saxophonist Eric Leeds, and drummer Michael Bland, and you—had during the making of this album.

Levi Seacer Jr.: It's weird, man, but we were in sync with each other before we met each other. [*laughs*] When we got together, it was kind of like, "I've been waiting to meet somebody like you that plays the way you do." When I first met Prince, he was an incredible writer, musician, and stuff. But the thing I was trippin' off of with Prince was, how did he get that sound that he had—from Minnesota? [*laughs*] When I first heard him thirty-five years ago, there was nothing but hayfields, snow, and cows out there. I didn't know how he was coming up with all that funk from a place where there was five months of winter and thirty degrees below zero. How was that happening? What were his influences? Did he go to church? Where was it coming from? That's what was trippin' me out about Prince. But when we all got together, it was like we knew each other in a spiritual, music universe. It was a breath of fresh air. It was like a musical Disneyland. That's the best

way I can describe it. We could do whatever our minds came up with, and Prince was game for that. He said, "I want to hear everything that is in all of y'all heads at the same time." [*laughs*]

You previously mentioned that he had a notepad for some of the songs. What was his writing process like?

Levi Seacer Jr.: Sometimes, I saw him write hits right in front of my eyes. I didn't know that was what he was doing at the time though. We'd be in the studio, and he'd say, "Give me a second." He'd be down there writing and writing and writing. He'd tell me, "Tell the band to take a break for about an hour and come back." So we did. I came back, and he had just written "Cream." [*laughs*] I asked him, "Was that what you were scribbling?" Because he was writing really fast. He asked me, "Do you like it?" I said, "What?" He was *that* prolific. He was like, "You know, I've been thinking of a song called like that. So it was just coming to me." When ideas came to him, he would stop heaven and hell to get the idea out of his head. What was amazing was, he would write it down, and when we'd come back from lunch, he had started recording the vocal already. I said to him, "Man, are you kidding? You just did that?" He responded, "Yeah." [*laughs*] It was almost unfair to be around somebody that talented. It was nothing to him. Nothing. He could've done it all day long. There were times where he brought in songs and they were finished. Sometimes, he started writing songs right on the spot, or making notes for the show. He wasn't keeping it as a secret. It wasn't like that.

You've discussed the making of "Push," "Willing and Able," "Daddy Pop," "Gett Off," "Cream," and "Diamonds and Pearls." I wanted to ask you about the three other singles that were released off the record, starting with "Thunder," "Money Don't Matter 2 Night," and "Insatiable." How did those songs come to fruition?

Levi Seacer Jr.: "Money Don't Matter 2 Night" was written in Japan. It was one of those four that we had to do basic tracks for. Now, lyrically, I can't say what his actual inspiration for it was. During that time, we would always talk about what was going on in the world and the state of our community. I would like to think [that] during that time period, those conversations might have been the inspiration for that song, because he felt like, what's the point of money? Don't let money throw you off-kilter. Keep your family together. Don't let money separate you from them. During that time, we would talk a lot about social stuff and the economy. He was very sensitive to those types of subjects.

"Thunder" was just a straight Prince thing. He came in with that. So your guess is as good as mine where that came from. With "Insatiable," on every album, he was going to have something sexy on it. He loved funk music and all that, but to counter that and balance the record out, we always had something lush and sensual.

Let's discuss Rosie Gaines and engineer Michael Koppelman's influence on *Diamonds and Pearls*.

Levi Seacer Jr.: Rosie came aboard after Boni left. Prince was a little leery about bringing in another female singer. He liked her sound, but he said, "I don't know, because I don't want to get used to it and then something happens." I used to gig with Rosie back in the day, and I said, "Prince, don't worry. Trust me, dude. I got someone. If you give her a shot, it's over, man." He asked, "Is she really that good?" I said, "Man, I'm telling you." He trusted me, so he flew her in. Prince said,

"I don't even want to meet her until she can prove what she can do. There's no sense in me meeting her and we can't get down." So he was in his apartment at Paisley and he said, "Levi, I just wrote a song, and I want that to be her audition. Take her to the studio and record her, and then bring me back the cassette. Then I'll tell you if I like her or not." I said, "Okay, cool." Rosie asked me, "Where's Prince?" I told her, "Don't worry about it. Let's go knock this song out." Rosie knocked that song out in twenty minutes. The lead and background vocals. I went up to Prince's office and he was eating. He said, "Hey!" I said, "Let me put this in." [laughs] I put that cassette in and he said, "That voice is in my studio *right now*?" I said, "Yeah." He said, "She sounds like Aretha Franklin, man." He was so excited. He said, "Okay. Hold on now. Is she going to give me a headache? Is there going to be a problem? Because I don't want to get used to that voice, man. I already hear her next album." You should have seen his face. He was so excited. It was like he got Aretha Franklin.

I said, "Man, she's cool. I already talked to her. It's all yours, dude. I told you. Didn't I tell you?" He said, "Yeah, but I didn't know it was like *that*." He was so happy to have a vocalist on that kind of level. If you looked at some of our tours, Prince would leave the stage for about ten minutes and let Rosie take over. On the album, all it did was open his mind even more on the possibilities of where he could go. The whole "Diamonds and Pearls" song, that was really him knowing he had a voice like that in the background that he could use. We had more of an R&B side to us than the Revolution. So all those elements helped to shape that sound. When he did "Purple Rain," Wendy and Lisa had a more pop [influence], like a Joni Mitchell–ish type of thing. Rosie got him into that soul and R&B sound, but Prince was already a soul singer. But to have somebody like that brought out that side of him more.

Remember what I told you about how intense Prince's studio sessions were? Prince couldn't just have any kind of engineer in his studio. First of all, if we were spending all those hours in the studio, Prince had to like you. He really didn't like people around him that didn't bring something to the table. They had to have some kind of vibe, because he was spending too much time with them. Michael [Koppelman] was a really cool engineer. He really knew his job, and he was musical. There were a lot of engineers who went to school, but they're not musical. They're coming at you with all these numbers and frequencies, but Prince was like, "Look, that sounds like bullshit right there. That doesn't sound good, I don't care what the frequency is. That doesn't sound right." [laughs] He only said that twice because, if he had to say it a third time, he was going to take a break and another engineer would be flying in from New York. Because you know, not to be mean, but he was like, "I don't have time for this. I'm trying to get this stuff done." Michael knew Prince's flow. Michael was really cool. Michael had a certain look to him, and he could handle Prince's temperaments in the studio. It wasn't like Prince was crazy in the studio. The only time Prince got crazy was if somebody didn't know their job. So Michael fit all of that stuff, and he was very musical. Michael knew Prince so well that when we were working, he was already fixing stuff that he knew Prince would fix later. Prince would say, "Oh, you heard that. Cool." That is what Michael Koppelman and Rosie brought to the table.

Michael, how did you begin working with Prince?

Michael Koppelman: After I graduated from the Berklee College of Music in 1988, the first studio I worked in was in Lake Geneva, Wisconsin, called Royal Recorders. I grew up in Grand Forks, North Dakota, so Minneapolis was always the big nearby town for us. So I had friends in Minneapolis, and I would come back to visit them,

because I was in the audio world. I literally called Paisley Park and said, "I'm a recording engineer in town. Can I come by and get a tour of the studio?" They said yes. And I went out there and the studio manager showed me around. In retrospect, it was hard to find people with experience on an SSL console, which Prince had in Studio A. Anyone can learn it, but the people who worked on those, especially during that time, were fairly rare. He was trying to hire someone, and I didn't even realize it at the time. The studio manager was super nice. His name was John Dressel. They asked me to come back and work for a couple of days as a tryout, then I would have a job after that, if it all worked out. This is what brought me to Paisley Park. I started at the bottom of the ladder. I was the assistant day engineer. I was aligning tape machines and getting people coffee or food, driving them around, or plugging in microphones, that sort of thing.

Prince was a big presence for a small person. I'd see him walking around every now and then. This was back during his *Batman* era, so around 1989 was the time I joined him at Paisley Park. He had a couple of big singles off that album. He was living large. Paisley Park was this awesome, immaculate place full of people managing a record label, wardrobe styling, soundstage, and multiple recording studios. It was such a busy place back then. On this Prince project, specifically, he was going to have one specific engineer and a lot of assistant engineers because he would work people to death. So they were always trying people out to see who would work well in that situation. Femi Jiya was the engineer on the *Batman* record. So they tried me out as an assistant engineer with Prince, and I worked with Femi. I don't think Prince really noticed me per se. There was nothing revolutionary about it, other than me not getting fired, because some people would get fired after working one day in the studio with Prince. [laughs] I began working more and more with Femi as his assistant engineer; then one day, Femi was gone. There were three main assistant engineers at the time. It was myself, Tom Garneau, and Dave Friedlander. We were all peers and friends and really driven to be great at what we were doing. Prince tried all three of us out at various times. I had no idea that he was looking for a new main engineer, but he would challenge us by saying we sucked. It would push us all. He'd say, "Put up the drum sound." One of us would be doing it, and he'd mic it. He'd shoo us away and tell the other one to try it. It was this bizarre situation. Tom, Dave, and I worked with Prince for years after that. I became his main engineer some point after that. I had a lot of experience, but it wasn't like I had the same amount of experience as Femi Jiya. Step by step, I kept doing more for Prince.

When and where did you first meet Prince?

Michael Koppelman: The first interaction I had with Prince was when he asked me to unlock the door to Studio A. But my first sort of real interaction was, I think I was the only one at Paisley Park, and he wanted to get in the vault, but he didn't know the combination. So he asked me. I wanted to be helpful, even though I didn't know the combination. So I called Therese [Stoulil], who was his assistant at the time, and I said, "Hey, Prince wants to get into the vault." She replied, "Okay. No problem." She began talking me through the process of opening the vault, and it was not working. Eventually, Prince began standing right behind me and staring at the vault door, while I was trying to open the vault over and over again. I remember him looking at me and saying, "Get help." The first two words he ever said to me were, "Get help." [laughs] So I called Therese back and eventually got the door open. It was the first time I said a word to him.

The New Power Generation. Photo by Steve Eichner/Getty Images.

The New Power Generation photographed by Joel Larson from *Diamonds and Pearls* inner sleeve.
(left to right) Tommy Barbarella (Purpleaxxe sampler, other various keys, and sex symbol), Rosie Gaines (co-lead backing vox, Purpleaxxe sampler, and organ), Michael B. (drums), Kirk Johnson (backing vox and percussion), Sonny T. (bass and backing vox), Tony M. (lead raps and backing vox), Levi Seacer Jr. (rhythm guitar and backing vox), and Damon Dickson (backing vox and percussion).

Being the engineer, you had a front-row seat to everything that was happening in the studio. Were you privy to any conversations that Prince was having about the direction he wanted to take his sound in for *Diamond and Pearls*?

Michael Koppelman: The song "Gonna Make You Sweat (Everybody Dance Now)" by C+C Music Factory came out in 1990. I remember Prince loving that song. I don't know what else he listened to, because I never saw him listening to music recreationally. But this song and what was happening in rap music *hugely* influenced him and made him want to make a record that sounded really big, fat, and tough. He pushed a lot of his songs in that direction with [rapper] Tony [M.] and layering out a ton of stuff and rethinking things. He'd have a song that would be done, and then he'd put new drums on it and push it in a whole new direction and try some singing or rapping on it, and then he might push it in a third direction. With some of the mixes at the end of that record, we had forty-eight tracks locked together of analog, just to mix all the various drums and loops he put on. He was influenced by what was going on in music at that time more so than I expected him to be.

He was always striving to show his variety, growth, and depth as an artist. When he was working on this album, was he working on his music alone, or was he accompanied by his new band, the New Power Generation?

Michael Koppelman: During *Graffiti Bridge*, I was his main engineer for that record. He was mainly alone. In my opinion, it felt like a low point for him. I don't know that for a fact, but he would come into the studio with his jammies on, and he always had his heels on. He'd come in not looking like the guy from *Purple Rain*. For most of his career that I was there for, he was *Prince* all the time. His makeup, wardrobe, and everything. The only exception was during his *Graffiti Bridge* era. On *Diamond and Pearls*, the band was there a lot. [Drummer] Michael Bland would be in the studio playing. A lot of the impetus for the songs came from that collaboration. Many of the songs were recorded live. Some of the songs were created and recorded in Japan. We recorded a bunch of songs at Paisley Park, and in London when he was playing at Wembley Arena. We had this large catalog of live tracks to pull from to create *Diamonds and Pearls*. A lot of it started with collaboration, yet he would have the band in the studio and just joke around and have fun and make music. Rosie [Gaines] was singing on many of the songs and around a lot. It was a fun time, really.

Walk me through what you witnessed in the studio with Prince's creative approach during the making of this album?

Michael Koppelman: I remember around Christmas of 1990 the record was done. He worked on it for another half year after that, so he kept working on it. I think the record company didn't want to put it out yet. They were trying to slow Prince down, which is a weird thing for a record company to do. He was frustrated because he wanted to work, and he wanted the record to be awesome, obviously. We spent the prior year working on this record, then we had to wait another half year before they would release it. I don't know all the details on it, but he worked on it for forever. We worked on every song for forever. There were a few exceptions like "Money Don't Matter 2 Night." It is one of my favorites. The song was originally recorded in Japan. He put on a few tracks on, and he put the vocal on, which was totally in the red, which made it completely distorted. Songs like "Willing and Able," "Walk Don't Walk," and "Live 4 Love" had multiple versions and sets of lyrics for. "Live 4 Love" was done probably three times. When Prince was going to record in the studio, we would set up everything: drums, bass, guitars, keyboards, and vocal mics. Anything he wanted to do, we were ready to do, basically. We'd put the vocal mics on the control-room side of the studio, and they'd hang right over the console. Then Prince would kick everyone out of the room when he sang. He'd punch himself in and out and we'd cross-patch him into a whole bunch of tracks, and he could hit record whenever he wanted. On "Money Don't Matter 2 Night," he pulled the mic up to check the volume on it. He said, "Yep, sounds good." When he was done recording his vocals, he called me back in. The needle was pegged to the right for the entire thing. It is something an engineer would never do on purpose. I told him it sounded good. I said, "Your vocal is totally fried, but I kind of like it." He had great ears. So, for this song, we hardly worked on it at all. It was almost what "Diamonds and Pearls" could've sounded like, if Prince and Warner Bros. put it out earlier. It's a great record. It was interesting to see the transition of it. It started off pretty sparse and organic.

Earlier, you shared that some of the songs were done in three different places: Japan, London, and Paisley Park. Can you talk about the differences between the three places and the recording process?

Michael Koppelman: I wasn't in Japan, so I don't know who recorded the songs there. In London, money was no object. Prince was performing at the Wembley Arena for ten days. He had a couple nights off between his shows. He booked studio time the whole time, but he couldn't get studio time at only one studio, so we spent two days at one studio and then three days at another studio. We recorded at some of the biggest studios in London. Each time, they'd fly me over there. Every day, we'd go into the studio to set up everything. The road crew would bring their recording racks in. The crew would show up, and we'd get everything ready. I'd always assume that Prince would be coming in, but some days, Prince would literally not show up. So we'd have $1500-a-day studio completely decked out and ready to go, and he wouldn't show up. [*laughs*] During the times he showed up, I remember recording with the band at one session at one of the studios. We recorded ten songs, but five of those are at least on *Diamonds and Pearls*. We just tracked a whole bunch of stuff, and I didn't know what it was at the time. A lot of the stuff was done in that one day in London with Sonny T., Michael Bland, Levi Seacer, and Tommy Barbarella. At Paisley Park, we were always ready for the band to come in the studio. The crew was always responsible for Prince's gear. He didn't have sequencers or anything like that back then. He just had his amps, guitars, drums, and everything else. For me, it didn't matter where we were. It was just fun to record in different places to get different drum sounds and stuff like that.

The main difference, non-technically, I think, would be that Prince was on the road. For Prince, being in a studio was his home. That's where he wanted to be, all the time, as far as I could tell. But the second best place was onstage. When we were in London, it was like playtime for Prince. He had the whole band there. They were playing in front of these adoring crowds. They had these suites booked out. When they showed up, it was fun. Prince was having fun. It was kind of a rare thing that Prince was not going to have fun, because he just loved working so much. He just worked all the time. In London, it was just fun. The whole band would come in. He came in a few times on his own and worked on a few things, but it was pretty much more entertainment than anything else. When we were working on the album, it was work, work, work, in a good way, but he would work all day long in London or Minnesota. It was essentially him trying to get rid of distractions to not being here. I don't want to make him sound like he was a sexist or something, but he prioritized women and music, roughly speaking, but the music came first every day I was with him, for sure.

How would Prince like his instruments set up in the studio?

Michael Koppelman: He would use the Roland D-50 for the keyboard controller, which we would have next to the tape machine. Back then, MIDI stuff was kind of new. I had an Apple—we called it a Mac Portable; it's like the world's heaviest premium laptop computer. So I was just starting to figure out what MIDI was like and how to record without a tape machine. But prior to that was a thing called Publison, which was like a digital sampler, and he leveraged the hell out of that thing. And it was sort of like the LinnDrum. It was a hugely important tool for him during the pre-sequencer world. At that time, before I introduced him to MIDI sequencing and stuff, I don't remember all the controllers. There was an E-mu sampler and some keyboards. All the guys would set up the guitar and amps, and we would mic them up. But there wasn't anything extra special. I remember some of the microphones that we used. For his vocals, we'd used a LeWilson 247 Tube microphone or an AKG C12, which was my favorite—we'd go to the studio and there would be two AKG C12s mounted to one microphone, or the 247. We set everything up so it would be pretty easy to start recording on anything. It was all analog, so we weren't locked to tape. So if we wanted to sample something, we would trigger it with an audio signal. Prince would be running the mute button on whatever song we were using to trigger the sample. He'd say, "Let's sample these vocals." So we put that in the Publison sampler, and Prince would play it on the keyboard and it wouldn't change the length of it. So he'd play it an octave higher, and it would still take the same amount of bars, which was totally revolutionary for the time. So he could make harmonies by playing the keyboard with a sample. So that's a lot of what we did. If Prince was going to the club to play a show or something and he couldn't be in the studio, he'd give us shit to do.

From your vantage point, what was the collaborating process between Prince and the band members in the studio?

Michael Koppelman: There would be two main configurations, if the whole band was playing. Prince would go into the studio side with them and just play as a band, specifically. Prince was out there, playing guitar and piano with the band, and very much part of the band. Sometimes, he would be playing in the studio, so he would be in the studio side with a guitar or keyboard directing them on what to do. This would happen when he had something that he specifically wanted them to do, versus the more like jam style, if he was out on the studio side. But otherwise, Michael Bland would go in the isolation booth with his drums in Studio A at Paisley Park, and the rest of the band would be gathered around up there. Levi played in the studio, and sometimes, it would be Prince and Levi in the studio. Levi was the right-hand man to Prince at that time. Levi was an amazing guy and musician and just got along really well with everybody, and certainly, with Prince. Prince respected him as a musician. But that was pretty much it. I remember—sort of side story—we were recording basic tracks for something, and Prince kept talking to Michael Bland through the mic by saying, "Hit them harder. Hit the drums harder." After the session was over, there was a dent in the snare drum probably the size of a silver dollar that was a quarter-inch deep, where he'd been

hitting the snare drum, in the exact same spot *every time*, as hard as he freaking could. I'm sure it sounded great by the end. It was amazing to see the precision and power he played with. He was literally beating this drum to death.

Rosie Gaines's presence is felt on this album with her lead and background vocals. What was it like working with her and Levi Seacer on this album?

Michael Koppelman: There were certain people in the camp that Prince really respected, musically. Sonny was on that list. Rosie and Levi were on that list too. There were certain people he wouldn't act like the boss to. Rosie was such an *amazing singer* and a bright, fun personality. Prince knew if he put her on a song, she would nail it. For example, he wanted some sexy breathing on a song. He had some girls from I don't know where hanging out in the studio, which was really rare. Let me emphasize that. He put them on the mic for fun. They were self-conscious, and they couldn't begin to pretend having sex on the microphone. The next day, he had Rosie go into the studio, and she fucking killed it. She nailed it on the first take. The contrast was hilarious to us, and even Prince too.

What type of studio routine did the engineers and Prince have during the making of this album?

Michael Koppelman: With Prince, the clock meant nothing. During my time with him, sleep deprivation was sort of his drug. And he didn't do drugs, according to what he told me, because we talked about it. He was Prince, so he could do whatever he wanted. On a typical day, we would start at noon and work until ten or eleven, and then Prince would go to the club and do something. He'd always have a girl with him. Then he'd come back at one or two, or three, and then work until whatever. In the presence of a girl, he would actually go home at three or four in the morning. Sometimes the girl would go home and Prince would stay, and we would work until noon the next day, or keep working the whole next day. Sometimes, he'd let me go, and I'd be driving home at three in the morning and my beeper would go off saying come back. So you couldn't predict anything. I think one of the reasons that Tom [Garneau] and Dave [Friedlander] and I were able to do all that was because we were young and indestructible. We could take the abuse of working all the time. We worked virtually with no food and we'd grab five to ten minutes of sleep. When Prince would go out to L.A., we could sleep for three days. When he came back, we started all over again. This was a project that never ended. It was hard work every day.

How was Prince constructing his melodies and harmonies for the songs on this record? Would he be by himself playing the piano or guitar and working things out before the band would arrive?

Michael Koppelman: Yes. It seemed to me that he did most of that at home. He would come in, and have a cassette that he would listen to from home where he played something on piano or guitar. He would walk in with the idea in his head. It was just a matter of getting it onto the tape. When he walked into the studio, you could just see it in his eyes and it would be done in hours. Literally, you could see it in his eyes. He'd walk in and the song would be done a few hours later. He did that with a lot of songs. Other times, he was constructing the music part of it. Then, he was doing the vocals. When he was out is when he would do the creative work of songwriting. I never saw

Rosie Gaines with Prince during the *Diamonds and Pearls* tour in Rotterdam, Netherlands, July 6, 1992. Photo by Rob Verhorst/Redferns.

him write songs. I never saw that creative process. I would see him musically exploring things with the lyrics and titles for the song. I never witnessed that sort of brainstorming in that area.

How many takes would he do when he was recording these songs? Since you said that he would sometimes come in with a cassette, with an idea, and then work on it. What was his process of working through a song from the beginning to the end that you witnessed?

Michael Koppelman: It's really hard to say. Many times, he would come in and start playing–just before the MIDI days–with the LinnDrum machine. That was like his old friend, in a way. I don't think the LinnDrum ever left his setup. He would be quiet when he had the song in his head. Sometimes, he would be playing boisterous and screwing with you specifically, or joking around with the band. When he'd hear the song, he went in there and point at something. He'd speak in this very low voice and just be focused. He'd start playing on the LinnDrum and get some beat going and grab the bass and do his thing. I could see he already knew what to do, but it was still a creative process, obviously, for him to figure out how to put that down. He didn't need to do multiple takes or anything like that, ever. I never saw him mess around. He would make mistakes occasionally, in terms of hitting the wrong note on the keyboard, but even then, he would fool around with the mistake and hit it a few more times, just to see if we were supposed to learn something from that. It had an impact on me. It was like, "Whatever it takes, let's listen to the tape," because sometimes those mistakes may lead you somewhere.

How involved was Prince with the mixing and mastering process?

Michael Koppelman: I would say if someone at Paisley was doing that, meaning Tom, Dave, or me from my recollection, he was involved to the end. I remember a couple times he let me mix things when he wasn't there. I don't think any of those made the record. He kept working on the songs, and he liked the detailed aspect of it. Many times we'd get to mix what we thought was done, and then he would come in and do some moves on the faders. With "Diamonds and Pearls," which was one of my earlier mixes for him, the first thing he did, he came in and grabbed all the reverb faders and pulled them all down ten decibels. When I listen to the song now, it's just soaking wet and there's reverb everywhere. When it came to engineering, he was always on a path of discovery. I remember when I came to L.A., and he'd been there in the studio without me. Prince rarely treated me like a friend. I worked for him. So we were at Larrabee Studios one day, and he pulled up in his car. He said, "Come here!" He played me something in his car, and he was excited about it. As soon as we got into the studio, he played it and the meters were barely moving. They weren't in the red at all on the mix. Sometimes when we would bury the needles on the mix, we were looking for what made the sound bad. We didn't care about the total harmonic distortion. Did it sound good in the red or not in the red? We would play around with stuff like that. He was in tune with every part of that process, even though he didn't really look at it like the engineer normally would. He wouldn't work elbow to elbow with mixers.

Levi, as you look back on the making of this record and the vital role you played in shaping the sound of it, what are your thoughts about working with Prince twenty-five years later?

Levi Seacer Jr.: I would like to say this, I can't account for all the peaceful times in Prince's life, but I spent a pretty good amount of time with him. I felt like his *Diamonds and Pearls* period was very peaceful for him. Even though he could be very intense, musically, I feel like he was really happy. I felt like we were really close as a band, not just musically, but like a family. There was a lot of laughter during the sessions behind the scenes. I felt like he was at peace with the world. I saw him smile and laugh a lot. He was really enjoying his music. I really want the fans to know that. There was a good sense of family and love during that period. So, I think, Prince will be a major influence from this point on, and he's always been, but more so now because he's gone. People need to know what excellence is and that is what he was. Prince was an innovator beyond music; he was a trendsetter in fashion and the way he used technology in his music. As far as religion and stuff, I think he would want to be remembered as a person that was all-inclusive. He donated money to many organizations and kept it secret. He really cared about people. I hope his example will open people's hearts, who have a lot of influence, to step up to the plate and use their power and influence to turn things around. He had a massive impact on me and everything in this life.

Michael Koppelman: It is definitely a source of pride for me. I remember when I had the master tapes for *Diamonds and Pearls* and I was taking them to L.A. I was driving in my car, and I stopped at the bar on my way home with my friends. Years later when I was in Australia, I was in this random place and I heard the songs from this album come on. I said to myself, "These tapes were in my fucking car." It was funny to think that I had the tapes for these songs in my car. It was just a crazy moment, connecting those dots. At one point, I said to Prince, "It must be amazing to know that your music is going to be heard by millions of people. It's a lot different than just playing songs to your friends." He replied, "No, no, no. It's more fun to play songs for your friends." It was a moment of wisdom. Ultimately, it was absolutely true. NPG were his friends and that's what he truly loved about music, more so than the millions of people that heard it, or the millions of dollars he made. ◉

PRINCE
& THE NEW
POWER
GENERATION
DIAMONDS AND PEARLS

THE NEW ALBUM FEATURING THE HITS
"GETT OFF," "CREAM" AND
"DIAMONDS AND PEARLS"
PRODUCED, ARRANGED, COMPOSED AND PERFORMED BY
PRINCE AND THE NEW POWER GENERATION

WB Paisley Park

As Prince took his fight with Warner Bros. public—for his freedom and his masters—he changed his stage name to an unpronounceable symbol as a direct assault on the record label, who owned his birth name. While Warner would temporarily shelve his next album, 1995's THE GOLD EXPERIENCE by the Artist Formerly Known as Prince and the New Power Generation would eventually be well received as an eclectic pop effort.

THE UPRISING

by Dean Van Nguyen

Artistry is about forward motion. It's that commitment to adding new brushstrokes to a body of work that can never feel complete or absolute. Leave it to the historians, chroniclers, and fans to gauge a legacy. While we're gathered here to get through this thing called life, artistry is going onstage armed with a purple guitar shaped like an unpronounceable symbol and "SLAVE" scrawled across its face because iconography matters.

Prince Rogers Nelson was serious enough about his artistry to give up his name. The Purple One had been locked into a marriage of convenience with Warner Bros. since the late 1970s, when the corporate titan joined forces with the Minneapolis teen virtuoso and gave him the tools to climb the highest peaks of Planet Pop. But by the early '90s, the relationship was beginning to lacerate itself, wounded by the indomitable beast that was Prince's own irrepressible genius.

Warner's plan for all its high-profile artists was set in granite: drop an album every two or three years, pluck a handful of radio-friendly singles, and watch the record hit *Purple Rain*–level sales. But Prince's mind didn't grind like that. The Kid was a relentless creative. His output couldn't be confined to the immovable margins of a company spreadsheet.

When one album was ready to be released, Prince already had a handful more in the chamber. His famous vault swelled with unreleased pieces. One of his many plans was to put out 700,000 copies of blues music free with a guitar magazine. But the idea was thwarted by Warner's executives, desperate to stop their star's enormous inventiveness from diluting his commercial viability.

"That intense creativity," says Michael B. Nelson, a trombone player in Prince's band throughout the 1990s (though no relation), "it was certainly at odds with how any record company would want to handle an artist and how they would perceive making money with an artist."

Prince urged Warner vice president of special projects for Black music Marylou Badeaux to talk her bosses into forgetting all common marketing strategies so he could release what he wanted, when he wanted. "I would tell him that it was counterproductive, that people can only absorb so much music from one artist at a time," she told *Billboard* in 2016. "His answer was, 'What am I supposed to do? The music just flows through me.'"

That a company owned and controlled his name—as well as any music released under that name—was also a point of contention in the public feud. Not owning his own masters tugged at Prince's purple lapels—his condemnations of the music industry became increasingly loud. He was one of the most gifted artists to ever walk the planet—more deity than mortal. Yet the Kid considered himself no higher on the hierarchy than a slave.

In 1993, the situation hit its apex when Prince announced that he would no longer go by the first name on his birth certificate, but rather the unpronounceable hieroglyph he'd launched into the cultural lexicon the previous year with the *Love Symbol* album. The funky emblem encapsulated the artist's virtuosity by blending the gender symbols for a man and woman with a musical instrument in a manner that resembled a cross. As Margaret Rhodes wrote last year in *Wired*, "It's impossible to know the depths of Prince's intentions, but the Love Symbol swiftly harmonizes ideas often in conflict—man vs. woman, sex vs. religion."

From the flames of the conflict emerged *The Gold Experience*, released on Warner Bros. in 1995. The first album to be released under the Love Symbol moniker, the music became lost in the crush of the battle with the label and blurred by the negative headlines surrounding its creator. Over two decades on, it remains something of a forgotten masterwork in Prince's 24-karat canon—a record that contained some of his biggest hits of the '90s but goes unrecognized as a fully functioning example of his relentless pop inventiveness.

In Great Britain, the heavy guitars and pub-ready melodies of Britpop were causing a wave of Union Jack–waving musical nationalism. The most popular albums in the U.S. in 1995 veered from Tupac's *Me Against to the World* to Mariah Carey's *Daydream* to a Garth Brooks hits compilation. On *The Gold Experience*, Prince looked to precisely none of the above. Here was one of the world's biggest pop draws, allegedly a half decade past his prime, flying above all trends. "I'm not a woman, I'm not a man," he famously sung on "I Would Die 4 U" a decade previous. "I am something that you'll never understand." *The Gold Experience* finds the artist once again recast as something the world was trying to get to grips with.

Get Wild

On the night of February 20, 1995, the Artist Formerly Known as Prince stepped out at Brit Awards at London's Alexandra Palace in a gaudy gold shirt, gold pants, and a cane to match. Triumphant in the Best International Male Solo category, it wasn't the flashy outfit that caught the crowd's attention as the thirty-six-year-old strolled onto the stage to collect the gong. With "Slave" written across his face, Prince, in that trademark deep baritone, delivered a seventeen-word manifesto that would summarize his mid-'90s mindset: "Prince, best? *The Gold Experience*, better. In concert, perfectly free. On record, slave. Get wild. Come. Peace."

In the tradition of British acts disrespecting Black American artistry (this was a year before Jarvis Cocker invaded the stage during a Michael Jackson performance), Blur's Dave Rowntree wrote "Dave" across his face. The silliness just underlined that Prince's attempts to isolate the mainstream was working. People thought he was quite mad.

"I don't care. If people think I'm insane, fine," he told *NME* journalist Andy Richardson almost two weeks later. "I want people to think I'm insane. But I'm in control. It was different before I became [the Symbol]. I didn't have control. I didn't know what was happening beyond the next two albums. But now I know exactly what the next two albums will be. I'm not playing anyone else's game. I'm in control. I don't care if people say I'm mad. It don't matter."

As Richardson tells me over twenty years later, "He wanted people to think he was insane. He orchestrated that. He used the Brits as a platform to say, 'I hate the record company, I'm a slave, they own everything, I'm just working for them,'" adds Richardson. "That's what Karl Marx spoke about when he said, 'This is what work is'—this is what we all do. But as a creative, it wasn't a satisfactory way of engaging with his audience or getting his music to his audience."

Among his unusual media appearances at the time was an interview with the BBC's *The Sunday Show*, when Prince covered his face in a gold veil and refused to speak a word to bemused host Veronica Webb. The behavior was another cruise missile being launched at Fortress Warner Bros.

"It was unfortunate sometimes when he did the name change, [because] everyone just talked about that," admits Tommy Barbarella, keyboardist and one of Prince's closest musical allies during the '90s. "Music and him as an artist were overshadowed often, at that time, by the name change. People were laughing about it. It was often hard for us to have to deal with that."

As for Warner's riposte, as Richardson remembers: "You only ever received from them a corporate response. They wouldn't get into a public argument with an artist because they could only lose in that situation. It would have been self-defeating. From them, [it was] a dignified or diplomatic silence."

Paisley Park

In public, the Artist Formerly Known as Prince was a chaotic madman. A twisted pop freak to be gawked at in the pages of trashy tabloids. But behind the outlandish exterior, *The Gold Experience* was born in a time of fruitful creativity.

Recording, of course, took place at Paisley Park, the near-mythical Minneapolis compound Prince called his home and place of work. In the early '90s, the place was a bustling hive of activity. Staff were on hand to address any needs the star might need. No minor errands were going to stifle his creativity when he caught a crest of inspiration.

By the time the sessions that spawned *The Gold Experience* came along, the number of people operating out of Paisley Park had been chiseled down, including the band. The horn section had been a key component during the early days of the New Power Generation. Rather than keeping them on a full-time basis, Prince would instead pick up the phone anytime he felt his latest joint needed some brass flavor.

"It was a much quieter place in the mid- to late '90s," says Michael B. Nelson, who had been a part of Prince's horn section since 1991. "Everything still worked great. There were always great people working there, but it wasn't the huge machine that it was when we first went there. Working on those later tracks, it felt more like his recording studio, and he didn't have that huge business umbrella that it did early on."

To outsiders, Paisley Park always felt like a workshop of dreams where the eccentric maestro inside would—well, it was hard to say exactly just what Prince did in there. Since Prince's death, it has become a site for pilgrims—a pop-music Jerusalem that fans visit to absorb the site where their idol did such remarkable things. As a workplace, Paisley Park was much like what they might have envisioned.

"There was always funky stuff," remembers Barbarella. "The studios were really cozy. The studios were full of scarves and tapestries and candles and incense and rugs—it was crazy. The whole place was used as a playground—it all changed every day."

At Paisley Park, there was no such thing as casual Friday. The Kid never looked less than music-video-ready. "He always dressed like Prince. Absolutely, I never saw him in any common clothes," says Nelson with a laugh. "In that world, it was amazing. Everything seemed right in Paisley, the way it was laid out, the way he looked when he came in. And he was always moving. He was moving fast when he came in when he walked by you. It seemed like he was always on a mission. He was always the Prince you'd expect him to be."

For the musicians, pinpointing the specific sessions that spawned *The Gold Experience* is tricky. Prince's collaborators never felt involved in recording an album, as such. Instead, he'd guide them through his sonic concepts as they came to him. As a member of the brass section, Nelson wouldn't hear how the fruits of his labor had been pieced together until he went down to his local record store and picked up the final product.

"In the case of all those songs—and the many, many songs that we worked on with Prince—you just kind of did them, and when the album [came out], you went, 'Oh, that's what that one was for,'" he says about the material that actually got released. For the other songs, "It went into the vault," Nelson laments, "or it was lost to history until somebody finally decides to release that stuff."

According to Princevault.com, the bulk of *The Gold Experience* was recorded between September 1993 and March 1994—around the same time material was produced for the album *Come*, which was released in 1994 under Prince's own name. It was an era that brings nothing but good memories back to Barbarella: "On a musical level, that time was really fun, because the band was really small. The band was always

Artist: The Artist (Formerly Known as Prince)
Album: *The Gold Experience*
Label: Warner Bros.
Release year: 1995
Performed, arranged, produced, and composed by: The Artist (Formerly Known as Prince) with the New Power Generation
Engineered by: Chronic Freeze, Ray Hahnfeldt, Steve Durkee, The Artist (Formerly Known As Prince), and Tom Tucker
Recorded at: Paisley Park, Guillaume Tell (Paris), and the Record Plant (Los Angeles)
Cover photo by: Randee St. Nicholas

Whole New Era

very good, but when you have a big band, you can only do so much. It's like a big moving truck. When the band got smaller, it was more of a lean machine that really could turn on a dime and do anything."

Barbarella continues, "Things got more and more unpredictable. As the '90s wore on, it became quite unpredictable. You never knew what was going to happen. He changed his mind a lot more frequently. He always did anyway, but during those times, it was even more unpredictable and hard to follow."

The Gold Experience was a shift away from Prince's early '90s new-jack-swing era, when he formed the New Power Generation to help him connect with a new age of jackknifing beats and hip-hop flavors. The album is instead a funky mesh of brash pop, fuzzy rockers, huge ballads, and futuristic funk. It sounds garish and expensive, textured and thumping, yet organic. An old-fashioned musician's album that moves to a sci-fi swing.

The grinding machinery of opening track "P Control" sounds like a swaggering swerve into a whole new era. It's rare to find a track this dissonant and still so funky. Prince's voice veers from a hip-hop flow to a wild yodel. In his opening lines, the Kid shouts out the recent drama: "This is your captain with no name speakin' / And I'm here to rock your world."

The message comes through in clear Technicolor: everything has changed, but nothing has changed.

The Gold Experience plays as something of a concept album, with tracks separated by segues depicting computer programs that can be uploaded into the listener's consciousness ("the beautiful experience," "the now experience," etc.). Prince was at the time tinkering with the idea of releasing music via the fledgling internet, but his plans were again halted at the request of music executives. Much like songs could magically make their way up your telephone line and onto your hard drive, Prince was pondering emotions and feelings being uploaded into the human mind.

Like many of his best works, *The Gold Experience* sees Prince run the stylistic gambit. There are scuzzy rock jams ("Endorphinmachine"), grinding funk workouts ("Now"), wounding ballads ("Eye Hate U"), and even a daft pop ode to aquatic reincarnation ("Dolphin").

"Shhh" sees the artist take back the slithering loverman number he originally penned for singer Tevin Campbell and turn it into a sensual power ballad. Opening with a rollicking drum loop that gives way for the singer's sultry vocals and seductive lead guitar lines, it's one of Prince's greatest showstoppers—a track that was still being slid into his live sets years later.

Michael B. Nelson enjoys the rare distinction of having a co-production credit on a Prince track. The sweeping dance-funk number "Billy Jack Bitch" ended up including one of the trombonist's own horn riffs. To stay sharp during time off, Nelson and the rest of the brass collective, known as the Hornheads, would get together and thrash out new ideas. From these jam sessions came an extended horn version of Thelonious Monk's jazzy piano track "Well, You Needn't," which included some original elements. Back at Paisley Park, one of horn players brought the piece to Prince.

Nelson remembers, "He even asked me, 'Who do I have to pay to use that?' I said, 'Well, you have to talk to Thelonious's son, I guess.' " In the end, Monk's music wasn't included in "Billy Jack Bitch," but Nelson's original composition features in the final cut.

The album's debut single, "The Most Beautiful Girl in the World," would become one of the Purple One's most famous '90s grooves. About eighteen months before *The Gold Experience*'s release, Warner Bros. yielded to one of their client's demands and allowed him to release the song as a one-off single through his own NPG Records, Edel Music, and distributed by Bellmark Records. Maybe their execs were tired of fighting Prince on everything. Maybe they hoped it would tank and the star would return to their doorway with newfound clarity. Instead, "The Most Beautiful Girl in the World," a fluttering '70s-style soul ballad that features Prince's floating falsetto, was a hit, and his only ever U.K. number one single.

The song would later be covered by Mayte Garcia, a young singer who danced on the *Diamonds and Pearls* tour and quickly became a full member of the New Power Generation. Mayte and Prince's relationship blossomed, influencing some of his prettiest ballads of the era. The couple married on Valentine's Day in 1996. Tommy Barbarella was invited to the wedding. He'd grown close to Prince over the years, though was still technically an employee. Getting a new glimpse behind the purple drapes was an unusual experience.

"I remember being there with him at the wedding reception out at Paisley Park," says Barbarella. "I remember posing for pictures with his dad and him. There's a picture somewhere of me and him and his dad, and I remember thinking, 'This is really bizarre.' Because I considered him a friend; but didn't he have other friends who should be at the wedding? I'm an employee. We were on the payroll. It was weird. The minute you started thinking you were tight like a buddy, sometimes you'd get fired. Everyone had their place. Tight as you were, it was a friendship in another way."

Perhaps no song encapsulates *The Gold Experience*'s gaudy greatness than "Gold." Built around a simple keyboard riff and a straight-forward rhyme pattern ("high" and "fly"; "sold" and "told"), it's incredibly simple, and yet gifted us one of Prince's most stirring anthems since "Purple Rain."

In the video, the band performs on a stage that looks like Oscars night if it was thrown by King Midas, or Scrooge McDuck. The Artist Eternally Known as Prince stands front and center. The Love Symbol looms largely in the background. Gold glitter rains all around, jumping up off the drum kit's symbol as it's forcefully whacked. Despite appearing to be shot in the runic ruins of an opulent lost society, the song voices Prince's freedom-focused mid-'90s mind-set: "What's the use in money if you ain't gonna break the mold." Everything he did during the period was an attempt to shatter all industry models forever.

A Vindication

The Gold Experience was released September 26, 1995, to solid reviews. The album sold 500,000 copies in the U.S., reaching number six on the *Billboard* 200. Lower numbers than a Prince record could expect to reach, for Warner Bros. it must have felt like a vindication. But the artist's mind had moved on to the next project already.

Rushing through the quick-fire release *Chaos & Disorder* to fulfill his contract, Prince eventually severed ties with Warner Bros. The 1996 album *Emancipation* was a celebration of just that—its three-disc format a wild declaration that Prince could release songs however the hell he wanted. For the remainder of his career, he never stopped testing new methods of putting out music. Prince may have gone on to have a strange relationship with the internet, but years before Napster hit, he was dropping online-exclusive albums, confirming his position as a daring digital futurist. In 2007, he finally fulfilled one ambition—releasing his album *Planet Earth* in the U.K. as a free covermount with *The Mail on Sunday* newspaper.

Freed from his contract with Warner, Prince began using his own name again in the year 2000. On the jazzy loverman ballad "Call My Name," from 2004's *Musicology*, he sounded happy to slide back into his former self, joyfully celebrating his identity through the lens of a lover. "I heard your voice this morning calling out my name," he sings. "It had been so long since I've heard / That it didn't sound quite the same, no."

In 2014, Prince regained control of his back catalog after penning a new deal with Warner Bros. that saw him release two new records under a renewed license from his old nemesis. It felt kind of perfect: the once self-proclaimed slave, who tried to reimagine the mechanisms of the music industry, returning to the corporate titans on his own terms. It was, perhaps, a symbolic validation of a battle in which he took his fair share of licks. For Prince, though, it had always been about the music.

"My music wants to do what it wants to do, and I just want to get out of its way," he told *Forbes* in 1996. "I want the biggest shelf in the record store—the most titles. I know they're not all going to sell, but I know somebody's going to buy at least one of each." ◗

(*opposite*) A 1995 advertisement for *The Gold Experience*, featuring some of the critical praise the album received at the time.

the gold experience

(4/2-45999)

- "★★★1/2"—ROLLING STONE
- "This is ♀'s best complete record since 1987's *Sign 'O' The Times*."—VIBE
- "A-"—ENTERTAINMENT WEEKLY
- "...His most effective and meaningful album since 1990's *Graffiti Bridge*."—LOS ANGELES TIMES
- "...Touched by brilliance."—PEOPLE MAGAZINE
- "...Among his finest works."—NEW YORK POST
- "...His best work since *Purple Rain* or *Sign 'O' The Times*."—THE CINCINNATI POST
- "His Royal Badness isn't rehashing his past, just rediscovering the essence of his genius."—USA TODAY
- "...The most potent hip-hop-rock hybrid jam to hit the streets in years."—PHILADELPHIA INQUIRER
- "...A winner."—SUNDAY REPUBLICAN

PRINCE ROGERS NELSON June 7, 1958 – April 21, 2016

Photo originally used for "When Doves Cry" 7-inch. Courtesy of Warner Bros.